CREATION'S DESIGN & PURPOSE:

The Front Line of Spiritual Warfare

CREATION'S DESIGN & PURPOSE:

The Front Line of Spiritual Warfare

GLENN H. KAILER

COLLEGE PRESS
PUBLISHING COMPANY
Joplin, Missouri

Library # 93-71345
ISBN 0-89900-616-7

Contents

Preface

This is a book on spiritual warfare. My ministry is in *Creation Evangelism*. "Creation Science" is a work of investigation, both of the natural world empirically considered, and of all creation divinely revealed.

I have been a full-time worker in the Kingdom of God for nearly fifteen years. I have held ministries in five states and presented the Gospel in several different sub-cultural motifs in the United States. Not until I discovered the power of the message of *Biblical Creation* did I find the key to the relevance of the Gospel to every part of American society with which I have come in contact. I now believe that the knowledge of God as Creator is fundamental to knowledge and correct understanding of God in every other role in which he has chosen to reveal himself.

As we, in the image of God, create, we begin with a concept or design. This design is the meaning or purpose of *everything* which follows. A builder who has no concept of the design will ultimately fail to meet the designer's objectives. A Christian worker who is disconnected from the fundamental order of God's design, reason, and purpose for creation can hardly expect to successfully announce, much less be part of reconstructing God's new creation.

The forces of darkness have set themselves to spoil the design of God. As in the days of Nehemiah, reconstruction had opposition. Today, powerful and influential men, even within the Christian community are either intentionally or unwittingly hindering the advancement of God's design being executed among men. There is a battle. But the Scriptures reveal that the enemy is not those persons we confront, but the *spirit* behind those persons.

We are at war. To understand this fact of the Christian life is to begin to recapture lost ground. But to fail to understand the essential underlying design principles in God's creation is to be ill-equipped for the battle front. You may have practiced spiritual warfare on some level for many years. I praise God for your commitment to this labor of love. But friend, if you have been shielded from the power which comes from a right understanding of *Biblical Creation,* you have been robbed of the full effect of victory over the prince of darkness in the battle for the *minds* of men. This book is my offering to warriors in the army of Jesus everywhere who are determined at any cost to present themselves at the front line of the spiritual war, equipped, prepared, and set on victory.

In the first chapter, we will see that the New Testament says a great deal about God's design. Words like plan, purpose, and intent all speak of design. In the next few pages, notice that God's design from creation underlies everything in God's universe.

CHAPTER ONE

Creation and Design

As I have studied and considered the implications of biblical creation and design, it has become increasingly clear to me that the heart of spiritual warfare is the work of preserving and advancing God's perfect design for human thoughts and institutions. It should go without saying that the work of restoration requires knowledge of the system being restored. But in the Christian community at large, as in the whole world, we find not only ignorance of God's design but apathy concerning the whole issue of creation and design.

Think first about the importance of design information in even a relatively simple restoration project. If one was to set out to restore an antique auto, it is surely possible to do much of the work of restoration by "filling in the blanks" from what parts are readily available. But at a point, there is no possibility of completing that restoration without consulting the manufacturer's design specifications. It may be possible to make the car work. It could quite possibly look good. But merely external restoration does not faithfully bring back from decay the automobile as it was designed and originally expressed by the manufacturer. Without adherence to the original design specifications, you may get a car, but it will be a different car than the one supposedly being restored. So perhaps you intend to improve on the original design and restore only the appearance of the original creation but now with a more advanced power plant. This may be good, but it is not a restoration. You have, in fact, created an imitation.

A good imitation with a faithful reproduction of the external body features may be a work of art. But to tinker with the heart of the machine absolutely requires one of two things: 1) The designer's own knowledge and skill, or 2) Knowledge and skill which at least meets or surpasses that of the original designer. Anything else will result in an inferior product. Nothing else has any hope of genuine restoration.

This principle is true not only of automobiles, but of everything created by man. If this is true of every complex system developed and produced by man, how much more would it be true of even more complex systems designed and created by God himself?

Many have undertaken to fix human systems, relationships and institutions without reference to the basic principles of God's design. This will at best result in a shell which may be a work of art from an external perspective, but the heart of the matter, the power plant, the inside is not a restoration of that which was created. It may work to some degree, it may be itself a noble work of creation, but it is not the system as it was designed.

But is this necessarily bad? What if the system is actually improved? The improvement of man surely is a noble work, isn't it? Any improvement in man, his relationships, institutions and societies must be a godly work, right? As good as this sounds, it presupposes this one thing: that the one doing the improvement has knowledge and skill which at least meets or surpasses that of the original Designer. Anything else will result in an inferior product. No one else is capable of genuine restoration. Unless you dare to claim more advanced technology than God, you need access to the Designer's own knowledge and skill in order to be a part of God's new creation.

The purpose of this chapter is to consider some of what God has said about his design and creation of man and his environment. Taking seriously these God-given design elements must be the first step in true and accurate restoration.

Creation Is God-Centered

There is no hope of restoration without first recognizing the Creator and Designer. John opens his Gospel by telling us, "In the beginning was the Word, and the Word was with God, and the Word was God. He was with God in the beginning.

Through him all things were made; without him nothing was made that has been made."[1]

There are people who profess to be Christians who believe that an understanding of "Creation Science" (knowledge of creation) is not an important part of the Gospel. Yet, John makes it very plain that the very possibility of becoming a child of God is related to accepting or receiving Jesus, the Word made flesh, as the Creator of everything which has been made.

The Apostle Paul writes to the Colossians about the centrality of Jesus in the same way. "For by him all things were created: things in heaven and on earth, visible and invisible, whether thrones or powers or rulers or authorities; all things were created by him and for him."[2]

In Revelation, John reports the theme of celebration in the very throne room of heaven is the fact of creation. Day and night, the elders before the throne give glory, honor and thanks to the Eternal One saying, "You are worthy, our Lord and God, to receive glory and honor and power, for you created all things, and by your will they were created and have their being."[3]

From the beginning of creation to the consummation of the will and purpose of God, his role as Creator is the basis for his entire relationship to his creation. If the absolute truth of creation by God is in any way compromised, no benefit we hope to derive from him is certain. No work of man has any foundation. We cannot know what is right, good, proper or meaningful in any absolute way. Our lives have no hope, meaning or purpose.

The Unchanging Nature of God's Design

Once we recognize the principle of God's "Design and Creation" as basic to who he is and what he is doing, we can understand that his ultimate objective for all creation is unchanged from the beginning through all eternity. God fully intended for us to know with conviction that his purposes are not open to reevaluation and adjustment. "Because God wanted to make the unchanging nature of his purpose very clear to the heirs of what was promised. . . ."[4]

God has not only a purpose for creation in general, but his

purpose focuses on us specifically. We who are pledged to become heirs of the Father are to receive an inheritance designed and established from the very beginning. This is clear from Jesus' description of the final invitation to the redeemed. "Then the King will say to those on his right, 'Come, you who are blessed by my Father; take your inheritance, the kingdom prepared for you since the creation of the world.'"[5]

To know the design of God is to prepare for our inheritance. But how can a man really know the mind of God? There is only one answer to this question. Jesus is the model Son of Man living in knowledge of creation design. He not only shows us how to live in this knowledge, but also demonstrates his victory over the world to the point of resurrection and glorification.

We have been given a unique window open to the intimate relationship between Jesus, the perfect man, and the mind of the eternal God. When Jesus spent his last night before his arrest in prayer, he spoke in terms of his confidence in God's unchanging eternal purpose and God's perfect love for him. "Father, I want those you have given me to be with me where I am, and to see my glory, the glory you have given me because you loved me before the creation of the world."[6]

Isn't it really obvious, not just from Jesus' prayer, but from common experience that the only reason for completely trusting and obeying the Father is knowing and believing the love of God? Paul describes the Gospel as a new kind of relationship with God offered to all nations, a relationship of obedience based on trust.[7]

What makes this idea so exciting is when you compare it with the old kind of relationship we all used to have with God. This obedience of faith replaces the shallow, superficial obedience motivated by fear. Jewish obedience was primarily motivated by fear of punishment. Gentile mythologies and superstitions are all fanciful explanations of fearful phenomena which make reality somehow subject to man. These myths eventually become guides to human behavior and decisions respecting their accountability (or the lack of it) to "the gods."

Knowing God's design and eternal purpose to be one of love leads men to trust him and obey (conform to his design) understanding that the objective of the new creation being completed

— we call it restoration — is to once again enter the *Sabbath Rest* in a glorious creation. "We who have believed enter that rest."[8]

Jesus, The Image of God

Jesus is called by many names in Scripture. One name especially relevant to our study is the "Second Adam." As such, Jesus is the original incarnation as perfect man, the re-introduction to the world of man in conformity to God's design specifications. Paul puts it this way, "He is the image of the invisible God, the firstborn over all creation."[9]

The whole purpose of Jesus' role as the Second Adam is/was to open the way to our restoration to the same design "specs." "He was chosen before the creation of the world, but was revealed in these last times for your sake."[10]

We who trust God and enter into an obedience relationship with him founded on allowing him to reproduce his image in us may confidently declare with Paul, "neither height nor depth, nor anything else in all creation, will be able to separate us from the love of God that is in Christ Jesus our Lord."[11]

The Restored Man
Restores Creation Principles

Christians generally agree that the life of Christ is a good model for our lives. But have you considered that Jesus, the restored man, gives us also a model for ministry? You see, he based his teaching, both in theology and in practical ministry, on unchanging principles laid down in the original creation. If restoration of God's design is the will of God, only teaching and ministry founded on the first principles of Genesis are useful in the ministry of reconciliation. This pattern of teaching was prophesied years before by the Psalmist. "So was fulfilled what was spoken through the prophet: 'I will open my mouth in parables, I will utter things hidden since the creation of the world.'"[12] The prophecy certainly pointed to Jesus' use of parable in teaching. But it just as certainly also ties his teaching to the beginning.

There are more direct examples of how Jesus used reference to original design as the basis of his teaching. When questioned about his teaching on marriage and divorce, he quoted Genesis, chapter 1, "Haven't you read," he replied, "that at the beginning the Creator 'made them male and female. . . .'"[13] Can we who are younger brothers of Jesus now prosper and neglect the design which he gave, defended and gave his life to restore?

God's Design Needs No Modification

I sometimes think that we who see ourselves as leaders in the Christian community often see ourselves as company *owners* rather than managers. What I mean to say is that we easily slip into the idea that by adjustments in our preaching, teaching or administration, we can better bring about the Kingdom of God. What is so deceptive is that this statement is almost as true as it is false. Adjustments are in order when they are deliberate shifts into conformity with God's design. Unfortunately, we are as inclined to quickly shift from God's stated design when it doesn't seem to work in our situation. Often the situation needs redemption to manifest the design.

Some will say that we've learned so much, surely things are much different today than they were thousands of years ago. But the truth is that God's design is not about to be modified to adapt to man's improved technology. No part of creation will redefine its own role successfully. When human body parts neglect their proper role as defined by healthy DNA and reproduce their own design, we call it cancer. When parts of the body of Christ neglect the programming of God's created spiritual DNA and express their own design, we call it innovation or creativity. God calls it spiritual cancer, sin. Sin always leads to death.

God's plan and purpose are not going to change or be changed by man. Peter described the purpose or design of God as being permanently fixed when he preached his famous Pentecost speech. "This man was handed over to you by God's set purpose and foreknowledge. . . ."[14]

Peter uses an interesting word here (or perhaps Luke uses the word to translate what Peter said) to describe the "purpose and foreknowledge" of God. The word in Greek is the word from which we get "horizon," a limit, a definition. It indicates that what God has willed is set, defined, placed and will not be modified. Every human effort to improve the plan of God is as futile as hiring a landscaper to move the horizon of the earth.

The Church Is to
Manifest God's Design Restored

It is by this same unchanging purpose that we Christians exist. "Now it is God who has made us for this very purpose and has given us the Spirit as a deposit, guaranteeing what is to come."[15] This is a completely new life for those who enter in. "Therefore, if anyone is in Christ, he is a new creation; the old has gone, the new has come!"[16]

We are expressly part of God's design and are to live our lives in such a way as to be proof of the goodness of the design. More than this, we are invited to become agents of the restoration of his design for all creation. Consider these excerpts from Ephesians:

> For he chose us in him before the creation of the world to be holy and blameless in his sight. In love he predestined us to be adopted as sons through Jesus Christ, in accordance with his pleasure and will—to the praise of his glorious grace. . . .[17]

> And he made known to us the mystery of his will according to his good pleasure, which he purposed in Christ. . . .[18]

> In him we were also chosen, having been predestined according to the plan of him who works out everything in conformity with the purpose of his will. . . .[19]

We can *know* God's design. God wants us to know his design. He wants others to recognize his design in us, among us and through us.

Jesus said, "Go into all the world and preach the good news to all creation."[20] The restoration of God's design is not merely a good idea, it is the event to be declared to all creation, for it is the event for which all creation is programmed. Paul emphasizes in Romans 8 that all creation is longing for our final victory:

> The creation waits in eager expectation for the sons of God to be revealed. For the creation was subjected to frustration, not by its own choice, but by the will of the one who subjected it, in hope that the creation itself will be liberated from its bondage to decay and brought into the glorious freedom of the children of God.[21]

James also affirms that we are the first part of creation to truly fulfill his purpose. "He chose to give us birth through the word of truth, that we might be a kind of first fruits of all he created."[22] He "has saved us and called us to a holy life—not because of anything we have done but because of his own purpose and grace. This grace was given us in Christ Jesus before the beginning of time,"[23] So, "put on the new self, created to be like God in true righteousness and holiness."[24] "For we are God's workmanship, created in Christ Jesus to do good works, which God prepared in advance for us to do."[25] We can do that, "for it is God who works in [us] to will and to act according to his good purpose."[26] "His intent was that now, through the church, the manifold wisdom of God should be made known to the rulers and authorities in the heavenly realms," says Paul.[27] Our privilege as part of the redeemed and restored community is to demonstrate not only to men of every culture everywhere the Gospel of God, but to demonstrate even to the unseen principalities and powers that we stand victorious at the front lines of the battle of the ages.

Endnotes For Chapter 1

1. John 1:1-3
2. Colossians 1:16
3. Revelation 4:11
4. Hebrews 6:17
5. Matthew 25:34
6. John 17:24
7. Romans 1:5
8. Hebrews 4:3
9. Colossians 1:15
10. 1 Peter 1:20
11. Romans 8:39
12. Matthew 13:35, quoting Psalms 78:2
13. Matthew 19:4, quoting Genesis 1:27
14. Acts 2:23
15. 2 Corinthians 5:5
16. 2 Corinthians 5:17
17. Ephesians 1:4-6
18. Ephesians 1:9
19. Ephesians 1:11
20. Mark 16:15
21. Romans 8:19-21
22. James 1:18
23. 2 Timothy 1:9
24. Ephesians 4:24
25. Ephesians 2:10
26. Philippians 2:13
27. Ephesians 3:10

Discussion Questions for Chapter One

1. In the Preface, Glenn states that, "A Christian worker who is disconnected from the fundamental order of God's design, reason, purpose for creation can hardly expect to successfully announce, much less be a part of reconstructing, God's new creation." Why would this be true?

2. In the first of chapter 1, "the heart of spiritual warfare" is said to be "the work of preserving and advancing God's perfect design for human thoughts and institutions." Does this make sense to you? Can you give an example of this kind of conflict?

3. How do you understand the relationship in John 1 between Jesus as Creator and the possibility of becoming a son of God?

4. How does Hebrews 6:17 (and context) relate to spiritual warfare?

5. Jesus, as the second Adam, used reference to original design as the basis for teaching. Would this be a valid approach for us? What would we need in order to do this effectively?

Understanding Our Warfare

War is never pleasant. War is the full expression of disagreement between kingdoms. Some wars are justifiable, even to the point of seeming necessary. It is unthinkable what could have happened at several points in history if men such as Adolf Hitler or Saddam Hussein were allowed to continue aggression unhindered. When all is said and done, the armies which overcome the invaders are celebrated as heroes once law and order is reestablished.

As we will later see, The Lord Jesus, The Prince of Peace is described as a Conquering Warrior King. His task is to drive out the raiders who have taken ground not their own and have taken prisoners and held them captive in an assault on the Dominion of God. The battle of the ages rages about us and within us. By the certain word of the Living God, the end of the conflict is already determined.

What is not certain, at least from human perspective, is the outcome of the many lesser conflagrations which constitute the war. The battle is between two kingdoms, both invisible, yet both manifested in the physical world where we live.[1] Because the war has a worldwide physical dimension, we are involved regardless of our understanding of the nature of the conflict. Because the real conflict is spiritual, we are dangerously vulnerable if not knowledgeable of the real war and how and why it is manifested in the physical world. The objective in this war, as in all just wars, is peace based in law and order. The question is *whose* law and *whose* order defining *whose* idea of peace.

In the first chapter, we saw that God, the Creator, expressed his design when he created the universe. The ultimate objectives of his design include glory, honor and immortality. When God first put his plan into effect, it was all very good. So what went wrong? It was an *enemy* invasion!

It all began with an infiltrator who shattered the peace by introducing doubt to the system. Innocent citizens were deceived into leading a rebellion against the status quo to their own loss. Because they had rule over all creation, the consequences of their decision impacted their entire domain. The design hadn't changed. Its expression within the created order had. From the first act of rebellion, the Creator promised to become also the Restorer. But this pledge of restoration was also a declaration of war against the invader.

This war is still raging. We cannot avoid taking sides. Every man will choose to rebuild or resist the Design of God. The key to this restoration, as was seen in chapter 1, is the recovery of the image of God in man. This restoration precedes the fulfillment of the hope of all creation.

This war is the war which fuels all other wars and is the only war which will end all wars. Your allegiance in battle determines your relationship after the conflict ceases. You will one day be eternally known as an overcomer or a war criminal.

In this war there are no civilians. There are only active forces, prisoners of war, or casualties. Since you're reading this, we'll assume you're not a casualty. Regardless of whether you are presently on the front lines or in the enemy's P.O.W. camp, you can determine to become or remain free, take up arms, and engage the forces of darkness in confidence of final victory. In the next few paragraphs, we'll consider what it means to take up arms. What equipment is available for the Christian warrior? What do we do with it?

New Testament Words for Warfare

Let's examine some of the words used in the Greek New Testament to describe our warfare. The first word is *polemis*. In common Greek usage this is the primary word for war and describes the declaration of open hostility between kings and their forces. The English word polemic comes from *polemis*. In English, polemic is used in a way which is consistent with the nature of spiritual warfare as it is revealed in the New Testament. Webster's first definition of polemic is "an aggressive attack on or refutation of the opinions or principles of another."[2] The declaration of *polemis* exists between God and Satan and their respective armies. Though we are involved in the conflict, the Scriptures never indicate that we have any part in the declaration of war or that we are in any way the principals in the conflict. We are seen as soldiers in the the armies of the kings.[3]

The Greek words for soldier, army and conflict are cognates, that is to say they are formed from the same *morpheme*, or word root, *strat*. It seems that the basic idea at one time was "to spread out," (like stratus clouds are spread out) subsequently, to encamp as in an army. The forces are those who spread out on the battle field. Each soldier is one part of the army and when the forces engage, the same word root describes the conflict. Paul uses this term when he says that "though we live in the world, we do not wage war as the world does."[4]

A third interesting word family is the root for both sword and conflict. The Greek root, *mach* in noun form describes a relatively small sword, perhaps a dagger which is used for both cutting and stabbing. The verbal form suggests the drawing of swords, or the engagement in conflict. Let's look at a couple of interesting contexts in which this idea is developed.

Jesus uses this word for sword when he says:

> Do not suppose that I have come to bring peace to the earth. I did not come to bring peace, but a sword. For I have come to turn 'a man against his father, a daughter against her mother, a daughter-in-law against her mother-in-law— a man's enemies will be the members of his own household.' [Micah 7:6] Anyone who loves his father or mother more than me is not worthy of me; anyone who loves his son or daughter more than me is not worthy of me; and anyone who does not take his cross and follow me is not worthy of me. Whoever finds his life will lose it, and whoever loses his life for my sake will find it.[5]

Jesus is using the word *sword* as symbolic of an occasion for conflict. We might loosely paraphrase, "I didn't come to bring the world into harmony as the world thinks of harmony. My coming and my message is rather the cause of division and conflict among the people of earth, even among those who normally stand in one another's defense." It is not at all uncommon for a person to discover enemies within his own home if he decides to sell out to Jesus.

This idea may be well illustrated by another passage in John. On one occasion of Jesus' teaching the apostle reports that "the Jews began to argue sharply among themselves. . . ."[6] This is the verbal form of the noun for "sword." You might say they drew swords — not literally, of course, but a conflict broke out nonetheless. This conflict was a direct result of division over the teaching of Jesus. "I have not come to bring peace, but a sword." This is spiritual warfare.

Endnotes for Chapter 2

1. See Revelation 12.
2. *Webster's Seventh New Collegiate Dictionary*, 1972, p. 656.
3. Note such passages as Revelation 12:7 and Revelation 19:11, 19.
4. 2 Corinthians 10:3
5. Matthew 10:34-39
6. John 6:52

Discussion Questions for Chapter Two

1. How is peace dependent on law and order?

2. Are there different meanings for peace?

3. How does one's idea of peace affect one's idea of proper law and order?

4. How is Webster's Dictionary definition of polemic like/unlike the notion of spiritual warfare as we are reading here?

5. How is this like/unlike other things you've heard or read on the subject of spiritual warfare?

Equipping for Warfare

In the previous chapter, we discussed New Testament warfare terminology. Now we will turn our attention to the weapons of our warfare. When Paul calls these also "weapons of righteousness,"[1] he is using the word *hoplon*. *Hoplon* can be used to describe any tool of warfare, either offensive or defensive. We have an English word "hoplite" to describe a heavily armed infantry soldier. (Yes, hoplite really is an English word.)

Panoplia, our "full armor of God," describes a complete set of instruments used in defensive or offensive warfare.[2] In English, the word "panoply" can be used in the same way. Let's consider each specifically listed *hoplon* in the Christian's *panoplia*.

> Finally, be strong in the Lord and in his mighty power. Put on the full armor [*panoplia*] of God so that you can take your stand against the devil's schemes. For our struggle is not against flesh and blood, but against the rulers, against the authorities, against the powers of this dark world and against the spiritual forces of evil in the heavenly realms. Therefore put on the full armor [*panoplia*] of God, so that when the day of evil comes, you may be able to stand your ground, and after you have done everything, to stand. Stand firm then, with the belt of truth buckled around your waist, with the breastplate [*thorax*] of righteousness in place, and with your feet fitted with the readiness that comes from the gospel of peace. In addition to all this, take up the shield [*thureos*] of faith, with which you can extinguish all the flaming arrows of the evil one. Take the helmet [*perikephalaia*] of salvation and the sword [*machaira*] of the Spirit, which is the word of God.[3]

The Belt of Truth

There is no word for "belt" in the Greek text. What the text says is, quite literally, "Have your reproductive organs wrapped in, or protected by, reality." Since the warfare is spiritual, so are the defenses. "Truth" in Greek is the word *aletheia* which indicates not merely that which is not false, but that which is really real, ultimate reality. As soldiers in the army of Christ, we set the standard for the thinking of others about the nature of our army and our General. We reproduce our attitudes concerning allegiance to the King, the importance of the battle and our confidence in our cause with every contact. We influence attitudes among our comrades in arms as well as among enemy troops. The thoughts, attitudes and behaviors which we help to reproduce are either according to the Truth or they are deceptive, false and futile. The only protection is to be wrapped up in Reality. Many believe this to be a result of being immersed in the Holy Spirit. At any rate, it is imperative that a Christian warrior know Truth, stand for Truth and reproduce Truth.

The Breastplate of Righteousness

Thoracic surgery is that involving the heart or lungs. The Greek word *thorax* is a *hoplon* made to cover these vital organs of circulation and respiration. Most people recognize the difference between life and death as whether or not a person is breathing or his heart is beating. Righteousness protects the vital organs of our spirits. The warrior whose covering is missing in this area is exposed to the enemy in a primary target zone. As important as righteousness is, it is easy to understand why we see so much confusion as to what righteousness really is. Since true righteousness is the only stuff of which a genuine and effective spiritual breastplate is made, we had better check the materials in our equipment.

Our word "righteousness" translates the Greek term, *dikaiosune*. It could also be translated "justification" or "alignment." When a typesetter justifies the margins, the characters at the ends of the lines are neatly aligned along the left and right margins. When God justifies the sinner, his life is aligned with the will of God. Isn't this really a simple way to approach the whole issue of righteousness? Who could be more righteous than the one who conforms to God's purpose? Our relationship to God, the Source of our life is protected by conforming to his purpose. The breastplate of righteousness is a picture of the covering God gives to the trusting and obedient believer.

Shoes of Readiness

Soldiers at the front need to keep protective footgear in place for instant troop movement. This footgear is described as "having been prepared in the good news of peace." As we previously noted, this is not peace as the world seeks. True peace exists when all creation is realigned with the will of its Designer. The Gospel is the proclamation of this peace, the only peace worth fighting for and the only peace God seeks to establish. I hope to convince you through the course of this study that any Christian not in touch with *Biblical Creation* principles is *unprepared* for action where the battle truly rages.

Shield of Faith

The *thureos* is a *hoplon* designed as an overall covering. The Roman soldiers of Paul's time carried a fairly long, oblong shield which was capable of providing head-to-foot protection from enemy projectiles. In a real sense, the shield was a protective covering even for the other pieces of armor. In a spiritual sense, without faith, we spoil our righteousness. And who can claim to be ready with the Gospel who has lost faith? If faith is the essence of our relationship with God, who can claim to be enveloped in Truth who is faithless? This faith, Paul says, is the very *hoplon* by which we "can extinguish all the flaming arrows of the evil one." We'll look at these arrows in chapter 7, "Enemy Activity."

Helmet of Salvation

Perikephalaia is a compound word which means "around the head." This helmet pertains to salvation. The helmet is protection for the head. The head is not only the center of our thought life, but is the control center for the coordinated function of every other body member. The protection God gives for the way we think and direct our lives is this helmet of salvation. Before we go on discussing the nature of the helmet, let's consider what we are to do with it. There is an interesting Greek word used here for "take." It's used many times for the glad welcoming of a friend. It is a word which means "to receive or accept an object or benefit for which the initiative rests with the giver, but the focus of attention in the transfer is upon the receiver."[4] This is not the same as just picking up something in the closet. This is accepting something God himself provides. If we look at a couple other places this word is used, it may suggest how to accept the helmet of salvation.

Jesus used the word *dechomai* as the way the Kingdom of God is to be received[5] and to describe the word being received with joy.[6] Paul arrests us with the negative aspect of accepting: "The man without the Spirit does not accept the things that come from the Spirit of God, for they are foolishness to him, and he cannot understand them, because they are spiritually discerned."[7]

Professing Christians who disregard the importance of *Biblical Creation* as foolishness are not in tune with good science nor are they capable of understanding re-creation. Having no grip on God's design in re-creation prevents full protection by God's power under a helmet of salvation. Paul also speaks of the failure to receive such things from God as refusal: " . . . they perish because they refused to love the truth and so be saved."[8] James recommends the proper attitude for receiving the work of God in his epistle. " . . . humbly accept the word planted in you, which can save you."[9]

The important thing in accepting the helmet of salvation is recognizing that it is installed by God. We are to simply and humbly accept it as his gift. What would head protection do for the Christian soldier? It would insure that his *thinking* and attitudes about himself, his army, his Lord, the enemy, indeed everything in all creation is based on the kind of thinking befitting one whose mind has been redeemed from every pattern not of God. This speaks of a restoration which transcends anything man could accomplish by his own desire or skill. This is that true restoration which is only possible when the Restorer has all the knowledge and skill of the original Designer and Creator of the mind of man.

Sword of the Spirit

This is a spiritual *machaira*. Do you recall what we read earlier about the *mach* word family? This is the same kind of sword which Jesus said he came to bring. Surely his sword was spiritual, too. How he wielded his sword in his ministry could well be a pattern for our use of this offensive weapon. Truly, the sword is offensive. As with the Jews who "argued sharply," about Jesus' teaching, so also our warfare will draw the lines of battle for many people.

The sword of the Spirit is, according to Paul, the word of God. What is this word of God? Many teachers have taught that this is a reference to Scripture. I really don't think so. First, if the New Testament ever calls Scripture the word of God (this, I think, is debatable), it would likely use the Greek word *logos*. Jesus is called the *logos* of God. This suggests that Jesus is the communicable content of God. All that can be expressed of God in time and space is demonstrated in the Person of Jesus.

The word *hrema* is used for "word" in this passage. *Hrema* is more often used for a specific speech act, a statement, a word, an utterance. A *hrema* of God would be a Godly statement or an utterance inspired by God. This utterance may be Scripture or not. It will certainly always agree with Scripture. But it will always be a statement designed to apply knowledge of God's design and purpose to the situation in which it is spoken and will often cause swords to be drawn.

Ready for Battle?

Paul tells us after we have the whole *panoplia* of God in place we should take our stand and pray. More will be said about the importance of prayer in another chapter. For now, we need to turn our attention to the battle itself. Few soldiers will remain in a state of preparation indefinitely if there is no action. What do we do? What do we defend? Where do we attack? This is the subject of chapter 4.

Endnotes for Chapter 3

1. 2 Corinthians 6:7
2. Ephesians 6:11
3. Ephesians 6:10-17
4. Louw & Nida, *Greek-English Lexicon of the New Testament Based on Semantic Domains,* United Bible Societies, 1989, p. 572.
5. Mark 10:15
6. Luke 8:13
7. 1 Corinthians 2:14
8. 2 Thessalonians 2:10
9. James 1:21

Discussion Questions for Chapter Three

1. Is there anything in the book's description of the armor of God that strikes you as particularly useful or practical?

2. How does this discussion of Jesus' sword affect your understanding of "The Sword of the Spirit?"

3. What is "true righteousness"?

4. How does the "helmet of salvation" protect our thinking?

5. Can a Christian stand in the battle missing pieces of armor?

Strategy for Warfare

O.K. So you're ready for warfare. Now what? You can't just stand around in your armor all day with nowhere to go. Solomon writes, "A wise man attacks the city of the mighty and pulls down the stronghold in which they trust."[1] If we're prepared and if we're wise, we're ready to move out. This Scripture may be what Paul was thinking about when he wrote to the Christians in Corinth about spiritual warfare:

> For though we live in the world, we do not wage war as the world does. The weapons we fight with are not the weapons of the world. On the contrary, they have divine power to demolish strongholds. We demolish arguments and every pretension that sets itself up against the knowledge of God, and we take captive every thought to make it obedient to Christ.[2]

As we touched on in our earlier discussion of our warfare, Paul uses in this passage the word for soldiering activity rather than the general word for war. We might read it this way, "We don't do what worldly soldiers do." Paul is talking about the nature and purpose of our weapons and our objective in battle.

Divine Power

Our weapons are of a type that their power is not related to the muscles in the arm, the speed of the feet or the force behind our effort. Our weapons are divinely empowered. God's weapons used God's way in God's service will accomplish God's purposes with supernatural power. This power from God is entrusted into our hands for the demolition of strongholds. Demolition I understand. How do I know a stronghold when I see one? Can I tell a good stronghold from a bad one? When do I swing my sword?

Identifying Strongholds

Stronghold translates the Greek word, *ochuroma*. *Ochuroma* is a military term for a fortified place, a fortress. Since we don't do what worldly soldiers do, the fortresses we attack must be different fortresses. To understand what Paul means, let's consider the basic function of a fortress. In the ancient world, a fortress might have been a castle, a place of residence for the monarch, the source of direction for the king's forces. A fortress could be understood to be a place of protection for the purpose of defense. Since we are in the business of demolishing these fortresses, they must be the intimidating structures built for the defense of our enemies, that is, the enemies of God.

In this spiritual war, the enemy's defense must mean protection from our offensive weaponry. What is the strongest, toughest, mightiest, most intimidating defense of the enemy to the message of God? I believe it is the philosophical structure of evolutionism. The apparent strength of this false philosophy has served not only as a refuge for those who desire to shield themselves from the truth of the Gospel, but has proven effective at intimidating and stilling the witness (sword of the Spirit, the *hrema*) of many Christians: "What do I say?" "How can I answer that?" "What if it's true?"

Some may object that evolution could not be what Paul is talking about, because Charles Darwin lived in the nineteenth century, more than a millennium and a half after Paul. Though this is true, it is not true that the world had to wait for a theologian named Charles Darwin to come up with this evolution story. One form or another of evolution mythology has survived the ages in spite of advances in science from the earliest periods in man's history. In Paul's day, Greek philosophers were promoting Plato's "Great Chain of Being." The idea of the continuity of all life forms and infinite gradation between them was common in Paul's day, too. I am not saying that evolution is the only stronghold in Paul's mind, but I am saying that it is a classic example of such a stronghold. More importantly for us, though, is that evolutionism is the primary stronghold of unbelievers in our time and culture. Regardless of Paul's idea of the greatest stronghold in his day, he would quickly recognize *evolution philosophy* as the greatest stronghold in our day. If we are in this battle, we can hardly ignore the mightiest stronghold unless we doubt the promise of God that our weapons "have divine power to demolish strongholds."

Demolishing Arguments

The notion of using the spoken word as an offensive weapon in spiritual warfare is not only a New Testament invention. Years before, God spoke to Jeremiah in the same way. "Then the Lord reached out his hand and touched my mouth and said to me, 'Now, I have put my words in your mouth. See, today I appoint you over nations and kingdoms to uproot and tear down, to destroy and overthrow, to build and to plant.'"[3]

The demolition of arguments is one of the activities involved in tearing down strongholds. It's worthwhile to consider both the verb which describes what we are to do and the noun which identifies what we do it to. The Greek verb, *kathaireo* is illustrated by its use in two other New Testament passages. In Jesus' parable of the rich fool, the man says, . . . "I will [*kathaireo*] my barns and build bigger ones."[4] Speaking prophetically of the destruction of the Temple, Jesus said, "As for what you see here, the time will come when not one stone will be left on another; every one of them will be [*kathaireo*]."[5]

It is clear that Paul is talking about a complete destruction by tearing down and dismantling. "With the help of true Christian *gnosis* (science, knowledge) he will attack and pull down the bulwarks of human sophistry [*logismos*] to the glory of Christ."[6] *Logismos* is what Paul says we are to demolish. The English word, logic, is closely related. But according to Louw & Nida, what is in view here is "fallacious and deceptive reasoning and, by implication, based on evil intentions"[7] Anyone who has carefully examined the walls of Darwinism, the claims for evolution, knows that the reasoning behind every proof strategy is internally irrational and designed to deceive. As to evil intention, there is no reason whatsoever to promote or defend evolutionism but the desire to deny God the honor due him as Creator.

Understand that arguments which serve as defenses against the knowledge of God are much more varied than just the blatant evolution propaganda to which we are exposed daily. The reasons given to avoid accountability and responsibility before God are as plentiful as people. Incredibly, even professing Christians "reason" their way out of obedience to the clearly revealed will of God. These reasons, though not nearly so high and mighty as evolution, are just as certainly strongholds which stand against God and must be condemned to demolition by the word of God. In another chapter, we'll take a look at how believers must deal with their own strongholds and faulty reasoning.

We are told that our warfare must include the destruction of "every pretension that sets itself up against the knowledge of God." Suffice it to say that whatever this includes, the objective remains clear: to make known the knowledge of God.

Suppose we do destroy these strongholds. Are we to leave the field in rubble? As God designed the world in harmony and order, restoration of that order must include not only the disassembly of those things which oppose his design, but must also include the reconciliation of each element of creation to his Lordship. Paul continues in 2 Corinthians 10, "and we take captive every thought to make it obedient to Christ." Take thoughts captive? How do you do that?

Recapturing Thoughts

Aichmalotizo is the verb Paul uses to instruct us what to do to hostile thoughts in warfare. We are to make them prisoners of war so as to gain control over them. These prisoners are *noema*. The term could as easily be translated thought or mind. It identifies our understanding, reasoning, thinking and deciding machine or its contents. In the next section, we'll see what the Scripture has to say about the *noema*. We will understand that the invisible war is truly a battle of wits. The enemy's infiltration is everywhere and we must follow the battle to every zone in which the minds of men are held hostage, hindered from knowing and serving the purposes of God.

Endnotes for Chapter 4

1. Proverbs 21:22
2. 2 Corinthians 10:3-5
3. Jeremiah 1: 9-10
4. Luke 12:18
5. Luke 21:6
6. *Theological Dictionary of the New Testament*, vol. III, edited by Kittel, Wm. B. Eerdmans Publishing Co., 1965, pp. 411-412.
7. Louw & Nida, *Greek - English Lexicon of the New Testament based on Semantic Domains*, United Bible Societies, 1989, p. 351.

Discussion Questions for Chapter Four

1. Have you ever encountered evolutionism as an objection to the *Gospel*? What would have made your witness more effective at that time?

2. Thoughts and attitudes are very personal things. Can you think of some different kinds of defenses that anyone you know has used to defend an idea he/she wished to protect?

3. Is there any one thought or attitude in your own mind which might be different if it was really made captive and obedient to Christ?

4. Why is it so important to actively engage in demolishing strongholds?

The Mind: The Battle's Location and Prize

To this point, we have seen that it was God's original plan and purpose for the *mind* of man to reflect his image. His purpose in redemption is to restore his design in its fullness. In the last chapter on the strategy of our warfare, we read how the work of the Christian warrior is a work of tearing down arguments against God and reinstating the Lordship of Christ in the minds of men. That really is the location of battle: the mind. Truly, one could say that the mind is both the battlefield and the prize of battle. To win the war means to take minds captive for Jesus. The joy is in knowing that only as minds are controlled by him are they liberated to fulfill their design function.

The purpose of this chapter is to understand the nature of the problem of strongholds in the mind and the source of deceptive philosophies and high-sounding arguments which keep men in bondage. Paul addresses this issue very directly in the same epistle to the Corinthians we were reading in chapter 3. He says the problem is that their fortress is so dark that they can't see the light outside. "The god of this age has blinded the minds [*noema*] of unbelievers, so that they cannot see the light of the gospel of the glory of Christ, who is the image of God."[1] These blinded minds are the same things as the thoughts we are to take captive for Christ. Here he is talking about the thinking equipment of unbelievers. He says they are blinded. They are blinded by the god of this age. They are blinded to prevent the entrance of divine light. Let's explore these ideas one at a time.

Mental Malfunction

Their minds have been blinded. When eyes are blinded, they have been damaged so as not to work properly. Light, color and shapes are unaffected, but there is no perception of these realities. The unbeliever's mind does not work properly. I know that many people with high I.Q. scores are unbelievers. We're not saying that the brain is damaged. We're saying that the processes of thought are short-circuited to avoid recognizing God. Perhaps the easiest way to understand the way unbelievers' minds are short-circuited is to analyze how they work. We need to pay attention to the construction of the strongholds when we dismantle them. Let's look at just a couple of arguments as examples of mental malfunction.

Dismantling False Arguments

Let's consider a *logismos* from the pen of Stephen Jay Gould. Gould is a prominent, erudite evolutionist. He holds a Ph.D. and is a professor at Harvard University. He has written many articles and books in defense of evolution principles. The following is excerpted from a magazine article he wrote a few years ago:

> Well, evolution is a theory. It is also a fact. And facts and theories are different things, not rungs in a hierarchy of increasing certainty. Facts are the world's data. Theories are structures of ideas that explain and interpret facts. Facts do not go away when scientists debate rival theories to explain them. Einstein's theory of gravitation replaced Newton's, but apples did not suspend themselves in mid-air pending the outcome. And human beings evolved from apelike ancestors whether they did so by Darwin's proposed mechanism or by some other, yet to be discovered.[2]

This paragraph, like every *logismos* or stronghold, must be dismantled and inspected. On the surface, the argument seems strong. It is strongly enough presented to intimidate most Christians who have not been trained in battle engagement. Yet, if you can only hold your shield of faith in place until you get close to this stronghold, you'll discover there's no mortar between the bricks. These gates are easy to storm.

The first element in this structured argument is designed to win your general agreement. We will concede that evolution is a theory. On this foundation, he places a challenge: Evolution is a *fact*. Now, as if to deflect our reaction to this assertion, Gould detours on an explanation of the nature of science. Now notice that his explanation of science is good. The problem is that you may be deceived into thinking that what he says about science is *true* of evolution. It is very common for evolution claims to be surrounded by science. Don't let an authentic moat around an imitation castle frighten you.

Gould, having changed the subject from evolution to science, introduces a good example from gravity. Incidentally, this kind of creativity proves the genius of men like Gould. Isn't it a bit amusing to imagine apples everywhere suspended between tree limbs and the ground? What did the apple say while scientists were debating alternate theories of gravitation?

"I've fallen and I can't get down!"

Of course, his point is that facts remain facts regardless of how they are explained. Physical processes continue independently of men's philosophies concerning them. Who would disagree? No one!

In the same way, he implies, human beings evolved without waiting for Darwin or anyone else to explain how they did it. Now think about the analogy. Has anyone ever experienced gravity? Perhaps you have even seen an apple fall to the ground. Your explanation of how gravity works really has no bearing on the fact. The collection of facts is science. The effort to explain facts in a cogent way which allows for additional investigation or practical application of knowledge is the true scientific method.

Has anyone ever seen an ape give birth to a man? Have you? Has Gould? No! Rather, brilliant men with mental malfunction caused by spiritual forces devote their lives and talents to attempting to explain how apelike creatures in evolution never-never land did what apes are today incapable of doing.

Why Are We Influenced by Such Reasoning?

Why would anyone fall for this kind of argument? Maybe because it is skillfully and persuasively presented. Perhaps someone wants to believe the proposition. Or could it be that they are just not adequately prepared for the battle for the mind that Scripture so clearly warns us about? Do you see how we dismantled the *logismos* (false argument) and exposed its deceptive nature? This can be done with every stronghold when we approach it clothed in the full armor of God and begin to jab it with the sword of the Spirit. We look for vulnerability in the stronghold and tear it down in the Name of Our Lord.

Let's take another look at some elements of a stronghold which reveal its inherent instability. We'll turn to the *Origin of the Species* by Charles Darwin and review just a few excerpts to expose the flawed reasoning which serves as its foundation. Take, for example, within the very introduction of the book, Darwin confesses:

> I am well aware that scarcely a single point is discussed in this volume on which facts cannot be adduced, often leading to conclusions directly opposite to those at which I have arrived.[3]

This is as good a place as any to point out that it has been maintained that every proof for evolution is a better proof for creation, especially when the deliberately withheld facts are added back into the equation. Charles Darwin knew this to be true and, I believe, almost every evolutionist knows to be true. The problem is that their minds have been blinded to the obvious conclusion.

Still in the early part of the book, Darwin admits,

> Long before the reader has arrived at this part of my work, a crowd of difficulties will have occurred to him. Some of them are so serious that to this day I can hardly reflect on them without being in some degree staggered. . . ."[4]

Can you believe he kept right on writing? Can you believe this is honored as "science?"

Darwin knew that if the Bible is in any way true regarding God's creative design and purpose, his theories were absolutely false. "Some naturalists . . . believe that many structures have been created for the sake of beauty, to delight man or the Creator . . . such doctrines, if true, would be absolutely fatal to my theory."[5] Evolutionists everywhere fight the notion of design or purpose of any sort in nature. It is a mental malfunction, indeed, to engage in scientific method on the basis of consistency and predictability due to the obvious design in nature and to deny the possibility that the obvious might be real.

Before we leave Darwin, let's look at one more illustration of self-delusion:

> To suppose that the eye with all its inimitable contrivances for adjusting the focus to different distances, for admitting different amounts of light and for the correction of spherical and chromatic aberration, could have been formed by natural selection, seems, I freely confess, absurd in the highest degree . . . . Reason [logismos] tells me that if numerous gradations from a simple and imperfect eye to one complex and perfect eye can be shown to exist, each grade being useful to its possessor, as is certainly the case; if further, the eye ever varies and the variations should be useful to any animal under changing conditions of life, then the difficulty of believing that a perfect and complex eye could be formed by natural selection, though insuperable by our imagination, should not be considered as subversive of the theory. How a nerve comes to be sensitive to light hardly concerns us more than how life itself originated.[6]

Careful reading tells me that Darwin believed that if the impossible were true, the improbable becomes virtually certain, in spite of the demands of common sense. You don't need a science degree to recognize the darkness, self-delusion and mental malfunction in this kind of nonsense. Some day, perhaps, we'll assemble a humorous anthology of defenses for evolution. But, rather than going on with this brand of illogic, let's turn to something closer to home, the whole area of religious darkness.

Religious Mental Malfunction

Enemies of God are not necessarily enemies of religion. For some of my readers, the bondage and intimidation of religious strongholds may be much more real and personal than the secular fortresses of unbelief. Many church members are engaged in warfare today. However, they are not fighting for the liberation of minds to serve the Living God. Rather, many Christians are defending institutions and offices. These are as certainly strongholds which oppose the knowledge of God as are the secular structures we've discussed. Their origin is the same.

Paul is analyzing the religious stronghold of legalism when he says of the Israelites of Moses' day that "their minds were made dull. . . ."[7] To understand what was really happening here is to take a great step toward understanding religious *logismos*. Let's consider the greater context. Paul is discussing the glory of the New Covenant in Christ. He gives God all the credit for his competence as a minister of this covenant:

—not of the letter but of the Spirit; for the letter kills, but the Spirit gives life. Now if the ministry that brought death, which was engraved in letters on stone, came with glory, so that the Israelites could not look steadily at the face of Moses because of its glory, fading though it was, will not the ministry of the Spirit be even more glorious? If the ministry that condemns men is glorious, how much more glorious is the ministry that brings righteousness! For what was glorious has no glory now in comparison with the surpassing glory. And if what was fading away came with glory, how much greater is the glory of that which lasts!

Paul Concludes:

Therefore, since we have such a hope, we are very bold. We are not like Moses, who would put a veil over his face to keep the Israelites from gazing at it while the radiance was fading away. But their minds were made dull, for to this day the same veil remains when the old covenant is read. It has not been removed, because only in Christ is it taken away. Even to this day when Moses is read, a veil covers their hearts. But whenever anyone turns to the Lord, the veil is taken away. Now the Lord is the Spirit, and where the Spirit of the Lord is, there is freedom. And we, who with unveiled faces all reflect the Lord's glory, are being transformed into his likeness with ever-increasing glory which comes from the Lord, who is the Spirit.[8]

If we are to discuss this intelligently, we must review the historical account of Moses and the veil which is at the heart of this symbolism. The veil is introduced in Exodus 34:

When Moses came down from Mount Sinai with the two tablets of the Testimony in his hands, he was not aware that his face was radiant because he had spoken with the LORD. When Aaron and all the Israelites saw Moses, his face was radiant, and they were afraid to come near him. But Moses called to them; so Aaron and all the leaders of the community came back to him, and he spoke to them. Afterward all the Israelites came near him, and he gave them all the commands the LORD had given him on Mount Sinai.

When Moses finished speaking to them, he put a veil over his face. But whenever he entered the LORD's presence to speak with him, he removed the veil until he came out. And when he came out and told the Israelites what he had been commanded, they saw that his face was radiant. Then Moses would put the veil back over his face until he went in to speak with the LORD.[9]

Moses alone knew the Lord personally. His intimacy with God became such that he was unaware of the radiance of his own face. Aaron and the others were as terrified of the reflected glory of God in Moses as they had been of the presence of God himself. To make them more comfortable, Moses veiled his face so they would not have to see the glory. Of course, the veil is entirely out of place in the presence of the Lord. Moses neither wanted to shield himself from the glory, nor had any reason to hide his own reflection of the glory.

As time went on, though, the glory proved to be fading. You see, under the first covenant, humanity had no capacity for sustaining the glory of the presence of God. Moses' radiance got a recharge in the tent of meeting, but without a fresh visitation, the radiance faded. We may infer from Paul's insight in Corinthians that eventually, Moses continued to wear the veil even after the glory faded to prevent the people from discovering that it didn't stick, even in Moses. For Moses, the veil became a deception, a pretense that the glory was somehow inherent in himself. Further it shielded the people from the knowledge that the glory was not in Moses but was simply a normal human reflection of living in intimacy with God.[10]

To the Jews, this veil remains to this day. They don't see any glory, but know that it's back there somewhere. Though the glory is now revealed in Jesus Christ and only being reflected in ever-increasing radiance by those in union with him, they still see the veil. Their minds are made dull.

Not only Jews, but all people who have seen a move of God in a church or denomination are in danger of the same mental dullness if they take up the veil that allows them to pretend that the glory is in the institution or the preacher instead of following the movement of God. It is the work of the deceiver to keep men from seeing (and subsequently reflecting) the true glory of the Lord.[11]

The veil, Paul says, "covers their hearts, therefore, their minds were made dull, for to this day the same veil remains."[12] (The heart is the core of man, the home of *noema*—the source of *logismos*.) It is we who with unveiled faces reflect the glory of the Lord who are being transformed. We must make it our business to expose the fading—or long since faded—glory of all religious monuments to turn men's eyes to the true glory that comes from the presence of the Lord who is the Spirit. The knowledge of him is the essence of liberty.

Before leaving this line of thought, I should add that there are at least as many irrational, false and deceptive arguments advancing religious darkness as there are in defense of any secular cause. Space does not permit a review of them, but you can learn to penetrate and dismantle them in the same way as the reasonings we have already dissected.

We've seen in this chapter that the real spiritual war is a war fought on fields of the mind. To take captives is to win thoughts and attitudes for our King. We have learned how to dismantle a stronghold. We haven't done it, you understand, for the real strongholds are in the minds of men, and to dismantle the real stronghold requires the use of our offensive weaponry to penetrate mental fortresses on mental battlefields.

We have seen that enemy infiltration is rampant in religious mentality as certainly as in secular thought. If this is true for humanity in general, how much more certainly will the front line soldiers experience the drive of the enemy to disable them and take them captive! Our next chapter turns toward the assault on the Christian mind.

Endnotes for Chapter 5

1. 2 Corinthians 4:4
2. Stephen Jay Gould in *Discover* magazine, May, 1981.
3. Charles Darwin, *Origin of the Species*, Modern Library Edition, New York: Random House, p. 11.
4. *Ibid.*, p. 124.
5. *Ibid.*, p. 146.
6. *Ibid.*, p. 133.
7. 2 Corinthians 3:14
8. 2 Corinthians 3:6-18
9. Exodus 34:29-35
10. 2 Corinthians 11:3
11. 1 Timothy 6:3-5
12. 2 Corinthians 3:14

Discussion Questions for Chapter Five

1. What, if anything, is the difference between secular and religious mental malfunction?

2. When does it become necessary to expose the faded glory of religious monuments?

3. What kind of responses would you expect to receive if you tried to remove old veils (if they exist) to expose the true glory of what God is willing to do through your church?

4. If evolution claims are often surrounded by science as a camouflage, what would you expect to encounter as a camouflage for dead religious thinking?

Deception: The Enemy's Scheme

The Warrior's Mind—The Enemy's Prize

If you don't realize that active Christians are in danger of mental malfunction, you may be wearing your own veil! In warfare, the troops most aware of the enemy's P.O.W. camps are those on the front line. Every Christian who dares to assail the enemy will fight the war in his own mind. Indeed, his mind is the prize the enemy seeks most to win.

Paul gives us clear warning of the danger when he writes, "I am afraid that just as Eve was deceived by the serpent's cunning, your minds [*noema*] may somehow be led astray from your sincere and pure devotion to Christ."[1]

Paul is saying that our thought life can become so corrupted as to be ruined for the service of Christ. It begins with the same kind of deception as was experienced by Eve. An anatomy of deception reveals the enemy's scheme to spoil our usefulness to Christ.

An Anatomy of Deception

Every form and expression of unbelief begins with doubt. "Did God really say . . . ?"[2] Asking questions is not in itself sin, of course. In some cases not asking the question has led from deception to death. For example, if several years ago, some followers of Jim Jones had asked themselves one night in Jonestown, South America, "Did God really say . . . ?" they might still be alive and well. The same conclusion could be drawn regarding David Koresh and his followers.

What we are talking about is doubt regarding what God might have meant by what he said just in case he did not really mean exactly what he said. Eve knew God had spoken. The question was not whether the words came from God. The question was essentially regarding personal response to the words God gave.

James offers a simple remedy for this whole deception cycle in clear and simple words when he says, "Do not merely listen to the word . . . do what it says."[3]

If the deceiver succeeds in planting a seed of doubt, he then offers an innovative explanation of what God might have really meant when he said whatever it was he might have said. Do you understand that for this enemy strategy to be successful, it doesn't really matter at all what he suggests God may have meant? All that matters to the enemy is that he can distract you from the simplicity of what God said. If you are completely obedient to what Satan allows you to think is the word of God, you won't feel so guilty about the exchange. But Satan knows you're really obeying him or even yourself rather than God. Either way, you are not trusting the word of God. This is the essence of unbelief at any level. You have innocently, quietly and gently rebelled against the Creator.

To complete the deception, you employ human *logismos* to reason out a way to justify unbelief and rebellion. This is done best by people who really know what they are doing. This is exactly what happened to Eve. Eve was very aware of her mental capacity. She had never felt confused or had any reason to doubt her logic. The most intelligent people are able to devise the most persuasive justifications for unbelief. Our society even cultivates a brand of professional rationalizers. We allow scientists and educators to do much of our rationalization of unbelief *for* us. Most Americans cannot give a good reason for unbelief beyond "Science has proven there is no God." I am not saying that scientists and educators are necessarily engaged in deception. I am saying that the most dangerous deceivers are engaged in science and education.

You don't need a science degree, though, to be good at justification of unbelief. Many leading seminaries train church leaders how to explain away the simple meaning of Scripture.

Probably the majority of denominations and certainly most churches follow leaders who believe exactly what they choose to believe, no more and no less. "Has God really said . . . ?" is no longer the question. They consult bishops, commentaries and colleagues before seeking the counsel of God. Then they teach you that church membership requires submission to their authority. "Well, they do make it sound right!" Beware![4]

Paul says that this three-step process of deception is what happened to Eve and is exactly what happens every time the enemy assaults a Christian's mind. If the deception causes unbelief in any area where God has spoken, the enemy has won that skirmish. Depending on the subject of unbelief, one good deception can secure the enemy's victory.

One Popular Deception Analyzed

Again, the problem is not merely that we ask questions. The problem comes when we doubt something that God has clearly revealed. Just for example, let me refer to one particular area of doubt which has undermined more people's confidence in Scripture than we'll ever know. "Did God really create the world and everything in it in six days?"

Let's first recognize that there is no question about what God said. You don't need even a high school diploma to read Genesis 1 and know that the testimony of God given to Moses says "six days." These days are further described as cycles of darkness and light (commonly known as night and day) and "evening and morning." Anyone who can read can see clearly that when God defines the work week, he wants us to work the same period of time between days of rest that he did.[5] Do you know any labor union that will accept working for 6,000 years or 6,000,000 years or 6,000,000,000 years or even 6 indefinite ages of time before a day off?

Others have written about this obvious, but popular, deception. For an example, James Barr, appointed in 1977 to be the Oriel Professor of the Interpretation of Holy Scripture at

Oxford University, previously Professor of Semitic Languages at Manchester University, said this:

> So far as I know, there is no professor of Hebrew or Old Testament at any world-class university who does not believe that the writer(s) of Genesis 1-11 intended to convey to their readers the ideas that (a) creation took place in a series of six days which were the same as the days of 24 hours we now experience; (b) the figures contained in the Genesis genealogies provided by simple addition a chronology from the beginning of the world up to later stages in the biblical story; (c) Noah's flood was understood to be worldwide and extinguish all human and animal life except for those in the ark. To put it negatively, the apologetic arguments which suppose the "days" of creation to be long eras of time, the figures of years not to be chronological, and the flood to be a merely local Mesopotamian flood, are not taken seriously by any such professors, as far as I know.[6]

Ken Ham is another prominent author and lecturer who has addressed this very issue as well. He said:

> I believe probably the major reason that people don't accept the days in Genesis as ordinary days is not because of what the Bible says, but because of outside influences, because they think that scientists have proved the earth is billions of years old. And you know what? Scientists haven't proved that at all! But, you see, if you use that to interpret the Bible, you're starting with the theories of men who don't have all information who have assumptions that aren't valid, and you're telling God what he means. You can't do that![7]

A science teacher at a well-known Christian college who has rejected the word of God regarding creation wrote:

> It is apparent that the most straightforward understanding of the Genesis record without regard to all of the hermeneutical considerations suggested by science is that God created heaven and earth in six solar days, man was created on the sixth day and death and chaos entered the world after the fall of Adam and all of the fossils were the result of the catastrophic universal deluge which spared only Noah . . . .[8]

Do you understand what he's saying? "I know what God says, but did God really say . . . ? I mean, God did not mean what he obviously *said*. I know better because we enlightened scientists are now in a position to tell God what he *meant*." It's the same scenario used in the Garden of Eden to instill doubt in the word of God and ultimately to exalt man's authority over God's authority. If the enemy can get us thinking that the earth is really billions of years old, even if he can't get us to believe in atheistic evolution, he can get us thinking that God is very distant, perhaps irrelevant to daily living, and certainly not to be taken literally at his word. This whole age of the earth thing is one of the strongholds we often have to deal with in the minds of unbelievers — even Christian unbelievers. The only reason for Christians to buy these gap or long-day theories is to attempt to accommodate the foolishness of the world rather than tear down its false reasoning.

If the enemy can keep Christians deceived at this point, we will be no threat to this deception and Satan's dominion in the minds of non-Christians. No Christian will actively tear down the strongholds in which he himself takes refuge.

Erecting a Stronghold

The question has been introduced regarding what God meant. The deceiver has offered an explanation of how we might ingeniously reinterpret the word of God. All that remains in the three stages of deception is to employ *logismos* to erect a stronghold of defense against the true knowledge of God.

Sample *logismos* #1: "It doesn't matter." This is perhaps the most popular stronghold in Christian circles today surrounding this issue. Some use this reasoning to avoid spiritual warfare altogether. They are A.W.O.L. soldiers in the Lord's army. Others use this stronghold as a shield of defense against the claims of God on their own lives and may be classified as deserters. You see, if God is billions of years distant, we don't seem to face an imminent accountability. Many deserters go so far as to say that we who assault this stronghold are the cause of unnecessary strife and division in the body. When professing Christians begin to insist that defending the reliability of the word of God on this issue is really wrong, they are P.O.W.'s.

The enemy has them bound and gagged within a mighty stronghold of unbelief. The veil is securely in place.

Think through the danger here for just a minute. Since the Scripture really does clearly say that God did create the heavens and the earth and everything in them in six days, the whole integrity of the Word of God is at stake in this question. If God does not mean what he so clearly affirms in Genesis 1, what does he really mean in John 3:16 or any other passage of Scripture? If we can't know what God meant in Genesis 1, how can we know anything at all, since God is such a confusing communicator?

Sample *logismos* #2: "Let's just compromise." Not knowing the truth of scientific inquiry, so many Christians are duped into thinking that somehow the nonsense of pseudo-science birthed in hollow man-made philosophy demands that intellectual honesty acknowledge the myth of mega-years. Rather than investigating the testimony of the evolutionists, they assume that God doesn't mean what he says. "Oh, yes," they will say, "we believe the Bible is true. We just don't know what it *means*." If it doesn't mean anything, does it really say anything? This sort of compromise denies the data of true scientific inquiry and reduces to nonsense any straightforward reading of the Scriptures.

Those who offer such a *logismos* to Christians with the intent to justify their rejection of the plain sense of the word of God are rightly called "false teachers." Writing to Timothy, Paul describes teachers of false doctrine as having minds which have been "led astray" and as "men of corrupt minds." Paul later used the same wording to describe pseudo-Christians in the last times, "men of depraved minds."[9]

Hopefully, you can now recognize deception as the scheme of the enemy to spoil our usefulness to Christ by taking our minds captive for his purposes. But I don't want you thinking that I'm saying that this creation/evolution issue is the only issue at stake. I am saying, however, that this one issue is the *foundation* of many other issues. Once we have abandoned the essential nature of God's design and purpose as we discussed in chapter 1, every other form of deception and delusion can enter our minds with little resistance. Consider how powerless the Christian becomes when Satan robs him of God's true design and purpose in the following areas:

- Prayer. "Does God really hear and answer prayer?"
- Praise. "Could I really be pleasing to God?"
- Evangelism. "Could a good God really allow people to go to hell?"
- Salvation. "How could God really care for me, personally?"

These are only a few examples of areas in which we question the word of God and find the deceiver's voice speaking alternatives which God has not spoken. Our spoiled psyches are perfectly capable of constructing *logismos* to protect our inner man from the truth of God.

As we turn to chapter 7, "Enemy Activity," we'll look deeper into how his work directed specifically to believers is designed to undermine our security and confidence in our relationship to God and to fellow believers.

Endnotes for Chapter 6

1. 2 Corinthians 11:3
2. Genesis 3:1
3. James 1:22
4. 1 Timothy 4:1
5. Exodus 20
6. A personal letter to David Watson on April 23, 1984.
7. Ken Ham, quoted from "Back to Genesis" seminar, Olathe, Kansas, November 30, 1990.
8. Dr. Pattle P. Pun, *The American Scientific Affiliation Journal.*
9. See 2 Corinthians 11:3; Romans 1:28; 1 Timothy 6:5; 2 Timothy 3:8.

Discussion Questions for Chapter Six

1. What is the danger of asking or failing to ask the question, "Did God really say . . . ?" in different situations? That is, when is it dangerous to ask and when is it dangerous not to ask? What's the difference?

2. James 1:22 says, "Don't just listen to the word, do what it says." Can you think of examples of someone doing something they decided the Scripture must have meant and, therefore, did something other than what it says? Is this necessarily willful disobedience?

3. What are the three steps mentioned in the anatomy of deception? How is this illustrated in the Garden of Eden? In the age of the earth discussion?

4. Two examples are given of *logismos* (reasoning). Some things matter and some don't. There are areas for compromise and areas requiring steadfastness. How do you decide which is which?

5. You probably know someone who lacks confidence in one of the areas mentioned on the last page of chapter five. Based on the topic of this chapter, what would you suggest as a remedy for these doubts?

Enemy Activity

What does the enemy look like? I mean, how do you recognize him when he comes? After writing the last chapter, I feel almost like the problem starts in my own head! Remember, your mind is not the enemy. The enemy is described by the Apostle Paul when he explains that "our struggle is not against flesh and blood, but against the rulers, against the authorities, against the powers of this dark world and against the spiritual forces of evil in the heavenly realms."[1]

The enemy is *not* my mind or my thoughts. The enemy is the evil host who, under the direction of the chief enemy of God, infiltrate our minds, implant doubts and encourage reasonings contrary to truth. In chapter 5, we recognized that the mind of man is the battlefield where the war rages and that the mind is itself the sought after prize in the conflict.

In the passage above, Paul uses a different word for struggle than we've seen before. It adds another interesting dimension to our understanding of spiritual warfare. "Our struggle" (*pale*) could be translated "our contest." The word *pale* (pronounced "PAH-LAY") describes a wrestling match, a fight, a contest. Our warfare is close combat, an infantry war, if you will.

With this said, we can better understand the nature of the forces which we engage in such close combat. Even though the war is ultimately between God and Satan, the actual battles or contests we fight within our minds are against enemy pawns. The Apostles all lend insight into these inner conflicts. One thing about which the apostles agree is that there is a close functional relationship between the battle for the mind and the control of likes, wants and desires. This connection is so crucial to spiritual warfare that our own natural desires can become the agents of our destruction. Is it possible that you are aiding and abetting the enemy unaware?

Enemy Soldiers Within

Let's begin with Peter's comments on this relationship between our thinking, our natural desires and our warfare. Just to keep Peter's remarks in context, it might be good to remember that Peter himself said the reason for writing both of his epistles was "to stimulate you to wholesome thinking."[2] Clearly, Peter was concerned about the Christian mind. Now remember, it is in the context of stimulation to wholesome thinking that Peter says this: "Dear friends, I urge you, as aliens and strangers in the world, to abstain from sinful desires, which war against your soul."[3]

For the purposes of this discussion, our interest falls to the word "war." In this passage, "war" is obviously a verb. The Greek verb here is based on the *strat* root we discussed under Greek warfare terminology. This means very literally that sinful desires within us "spread out to take the field, serving as soldiers" against our souls (*psyche*, self, inner life, one's inmost being, person). It is immediately clear that our natural desires can be enlisted to serve the enemy of our souls.

Enemy Infiltration of Our Ranks

James explains that the internal conflicts within the Christian army are also the result of our own desires. To understand what he's talking about, recall some of the warfare terms discussed previously as we read this passage.

What causes fights [*polemis* - the word for "war"] and quarrels [*machairo* - that word for drawing swords we discussed in chapter 2] among you? Don't they come from your desires that battle [*strateuo* - serve as soldiers] within you? You want something but don't get it. You kill and covet, but you cannot have what you want. You quarrel [*machairo*] and fight [*polemis*]. You do not have, because you do not ask God. When you ask, you do not receive, because you ask with wrong motives, that you may spend what you get on your pleasures.

You adulterous people, don't you know that friendship with the world is hatred toward God? Anyone who chooses to be a friend of the world becomes an enemy of God . . .

Submit yourselves, then, to God. Resist the devil, and he will flee from you. Come near to God and he will come near to you. Wash your hands, you sinners, and purify your hearts, you double-minded. Grieve, mourn and wail. Change your laughter to mourning and your joy to gloom. Humble yourselves before the Lord, and he will lift you up.[4]

James makes it clear that desires (or personal preferences—another meaning of *epithumia*) cause conflict. He indicts wrong desires as the reason prayers go apparently unanswered. As he continues, he is really suggesting several other things we must consider if we will ever take seriously the threat to our security coming from within ourselves. In the next few pages, we're going to see that desires are not necessarily bad, but it makes a difference what motivates desire. Further, we will see how the Apostles identify natural human desires with a pagan lifestyle and how Christians are by definition fighting against the very things the world seeks. This is why James addresses "friendship with the world."

Desire Is Not Necessarily Bad

We have said already that desire in itself is not necessarily bad. Before we explore this proposition, we need to define some terms. The New Testament uses two different words for desire in the passages we'll study together. These words are *epithumia* (pronounced "EPP-EE-THOO-MEE-AH") and *hedone* (pronounced "HAY-DON-AY"). *Epithumia* is a pretty flexible word having to do with "want." Its meaning can range all the way from wish to want, desire to lust, longing to coveting. *Hedone* has to do with pleasure. It could cover everything from "I like it." to "It turns me on." "If it feels good, do it" might be the motto of a hedonist, one who practices hedonism, the search for pleasure. In the words of a recent pop song, "I like it, I want it" covers both ideas. The song might say, in semi-Greek, "It gives me *hedone*, I *epithumia* it."

Neither *epithumia* nor *hedone* are in themselves evil, though both tend to imply control of the flesh. As we will see shortly, though, there is spiritual *epithumia* in contrast with the desire of the flesh. The point is that the problem is one of control or orientation rather than whether or not we have desire. The same is true of *hedone*. Though it normally means pleasurable taste or feeling, even Aristotle taught that the highest pleasure derived from rational activity. He meant this is a virtuous sense. More often than not, though, when a Christian experiences true, Godly pleasure, it is called joy.

In Galatians, Paul addresses this idea of control as the source of internal conflict. "The sinful nature desires [*epithumia*] what is contrary to the Spirit, and the Spirit what is contrary to the sinful nature. They are in conflict with each other, so that you do not do what you want."[5] Clearly, we can either allow our natural desires to control our thoughts and behavior or we subject our thoughts, behavior and desires to the control of the Spirit.

We've already read words from Peter, James and Paul identifying desires as a root of conflict. We're about to see how this desire orientation is used by the enemy to keep people from seeing, recognizing or living according to truth.

Desires Keep People from Truth

Paul recognized a major characteristic of our times would be a search for pleasure, a "me-generation," an exaltation of personal wants. He prophesied that "the time will come when men will not put up with sound doctrine. Instead, to suit their own desires, they will gather around them a great number of teachers to say what their itching ears want to hear."[6]

Peter went a bit further when he declared that it was of first importance to understand that the scoffers of our days would be motivated by their own wants. He said, "First of all, you must understand that in the last days scoffers will come, scoffing and following their own evil desires [*epithumia*]."[7]

Jude was in agreement with Peter and the other Apostles in this evaluation of the coming times. He told us to:

> ... remember what the apostles of our Lord Jesus Christ foretold. They said to you, "In the last times there will be scoffers who will follow their own ungodly desires [*epithumia*]." These are the men who divide you, who follow mere natural instincts and do not have the Spirit.[8]

Desires Keep Christians from Being Fruitful

We've already seen that even Christians have problems with desire. But did you know that Jesus taught that these same personal desires were like weeds in a Christian's life, robbing him of the fruit of the work of God in his life? It is in the parable of the sower that Jesus tells how "the worries of this life, the deceitfulness of wealth and the desires [*epithumia*] for other things come in and choke the word, making it unfruitful."[9]

Paul also implicated the deceitfulness of wealth as an "*epithumia*-snare" or "*epithumia*-trap" in a letter to Timothy. "People who want to get rich fall into temptation and a trap and into many foolish and harmful desires that plunge men into ruin and destruction."[10] Every natural desire in you which remains dominated by the world rather than being subjected to the Spirit is a potential hook by which you may again be made captive by glamorous leaders. "For they mouth empty, boastful words and, by appealing to the lustful desires [*epithumia*] of sinful human nature, they entice people who are just escaping from those who live in error."[11]

Natural Desire Is Really
the Cause of All Corruption

It was when Eve reasoned that the forbidden fruit was desirable that she established the course of human history. It was Adam's agreement with Eve regarding the desirability of that which opposed the will and design of God which brought about the curse on all matter, which identify as the Second Law of Thermodynamics. The New Testament also affirms that all corruption, all decay, derive from human desires. Peter says that this is the reason why God "has given us his very great and precious promises, so that through them you may participate in the divine nature and escape the corruption in the world caused by evil desires."[12] This state of decay in every system is part of the Law [rule] of Sin and Death.

Paul suggests that obedience to desire is related to making sin your king. He says to the Romans, "do not let sin reign in your mortal body so that you obey its evil desires [*epithumia*]."[13] The word for "reign" is built from the same word root as the word for king. When sin reigns as king, you follow wants and wishes. This law of sin and death is further explained when he says that "sin, seizing the opportunity afforded by the commandment, produced in me every kind of covetous desire [*epithumia*]. For apart from law, sin is dead."[14]

You may right about now think we've really gone off track from our original discussion. Not so fast! Paul specifically says that this law of sin and death is engaged in anti-personnel warfare when he says, "I see another law at work in the members of my body, waging war against the law of my mind and making me a prisoner of the law of sin at work within my members."[15] This word for waging war is *antistrateuomai*. It is a verb which means to oppose the enemy forces. In this case, the administration of sin and death control the forces which are opposed to the forces of God. This discussion about desire and the law of sin and death is absolutely integral to a biblical understanding of spiritual warfare!

The very problem with the natural man, our Adamic nature, is that it is being wasted or spoiled by our basic desires which deceive us into thinking that what we want is good for us. Paul tells the Ephesians "You were taught, with regard to your former way of life, to put off your old self, which is being corrupted by its deceitful desires . . . ."[16]

Living by Epithumia Is the Essence of Paganism

John tells us that the source of natural desires is not God. He says that "everything in the world— the cravings [*epithumia*] of sinful man, the lust [*epithumia*] of his eyes and the boasting of what he has and does— comes not from the Father but from the world. The world and its desires pass away, but the man who does the will of God lives forever."[17]

Peter tells us to leave natural human desires behind us. "As obedient children, do not conform to the evil desires you had when you lived in ignorance."[18] He also says that once a person is being restored to the likeness of Christ, "he does not live the rest of his earthly life for evil human desires, but rather for the will of God."[19] Respect for human wants and desires and decision—making based on personal preferences are contrary to being led by the Spirit and will of God. It is human desires which cause all manner of bickering as well as the internal conflict mentioned by both Peter and Paul. Jude says of some divisive men, "These men are grumblers and faultfinders; they follow their own evil desires [*epithumia*]; they boast about themselves and flatter others for their own advantage."[20]

Even in the first century, immature believers were deceived into thinking that something outside themselves was responsible for occasions to sin. But James wrote that, "each one is tempted when, by his own evil desire, he is dragged away and enticed." He continued in the same passage to explain that our likes and wants (which have become virtually sacred in a democratic society) will lead us to death if we allow them to. "Then, after desire has conceived, it gives birth to sin; and sin, when it is full-grown, gives birth to death."[21]

As believers we are to conduct our lives in a holy way, "not in passionate lust [*epithumia*] like the heathen, who do not know God"[22] and, as Peter says, we are to give up living according to human wants and live by the will of God:

> "For you have spent enough time in the past doing what pagans choose to do—living in debauchery, lust [*epithumia*], drunkenness, orgies, carousing and detestable idolatry."[23]

"At one time we too were foolish, disobedient, deceived and enslaved by all kinds of passions and pleasures. We lived in malice and envy, being hated and hating one another."[24]

"All of us also lived among them at one time, gratifying the cravings of our sinful nature and following its desires [epithumia] and thoughts. Like the rest, we were by nature objects of wrath."[25]

We've surely seen that human desire is opposed to the purposes of God. Our desires spread out to serve as enemy soldiers against us personally and infiltrate the ranks of the Christian army to cause internal conflict, dissension and division. What we need now is to have some understanding about winning this part of the war.

So What Do We Do About Bad Epithumia?

Paul tells us we should "clothe [ourselves] with the Lord Jesus Christ, and do not think about how to gratify the desires of the sinful nature."[26]

He even tells us that the key to living in Christ is to "live by the Spirit, and you will not gratify the desires of the sinful nature."[27] "Put to death, therefore, whatever belongs to your earthly nature: sexual immorality, impurity, lust, evil desires and greed, which is idolatry."[28] "Flee the evil desires of youth, and pursue righteousness, faith, love and peace, along with those who call on the Lord out of a pure heart."[29]

Paul writes to Titus of our deliverance from these very things in these words:

... the grace of God that brings salvation has appeared to all men. It teaches us to say "No" to ungodliness and worldly passions, and to live self-controlled, upright and godly lives in this present age, while we wait for the blessed hope—the glorious appearing of our great God and Savior, Jesus Christ, who gave himself for us to redeem us from all wickedness and to purify for himself a people that are his very own, eager to do what is good.[30]

Some will say, "This is easy for you to say! I'm just not as spiritual as you are." Get your want-to's in line with the truth of God! Are you a Christian? Do you belong to Christ? The Scripture says that "Those who belong to Christ Jesus have crucified the sinful nature with its passions and desires."[31] The truth is that God has provided your deliverance from deceitful desires and instincts and has given you a new way of thinking, the mind of Christ. Live in the truth; you shall be free indeed!

Benefits of Spirit-Controlled Epithumia

Besides the obvious benefit of freedom from the world to live a life truly alive in God, we find an all new control center for our desires produces an all new orientation for our pleasures. When we desire the will of God, our highest pleasure is the joy we experience from the fulfillment of God's perfect will in our lives. When a man's desires are the desires of God, he knows both peace and prosperity. Psalms 1 tells of the blessedness of the man whose delight is in the law of the Lord and how whatever he does prospers. Paul writes in Philippians that "it is God who works in you to will and to act according to his good purpose."[32]

In another passage, Paul suggests that Satan cannot outwit us if we are aware of his schemes (noema). If we learn to recognize Satan's way of thinking, which includes focusing on human desires rather than the will and purpose of God, we will be prepared to defend ourselves in this battle of the ages.[33]

Endnotes for Chapter 7

1. Ephesians 6:12
2. 2 Peter 3:1
3. 1 Peter 2:11
4. James 4:1-10
5. Galatians 5:17
6. 2 Timothy 4:3
7. 2 Peter 3:3
8. Jude 17-19
9. Mark 4:19
10. 1 Timothy 6:9
11. 2 Peter 2:18
12. 2 Peter 1:4
13. Romans 6:12
14. Romans 7:8
15. Romans 7:23
16. Ephesians 4:22
17. 1 John 2:16-17
18. 1 Peter 1:14
19. 1 Peter 4:2
20. Jude 16
21. James 1:14-15
22. 1 Thessalonians 4:5
23. 1 Peter 4:3
24. Titus 3:3
25. Ephesians 2:3
26. Romans 13:14
27. Galatians 5:16
28. Colossians 3:5
29. 2 Timothy 2:22
30. Titus 2:11-14
31. Galatians 5:24
32. Philippians 2:13
33. 2 Corinthians 2:11

Discussion Questions for Chapter Seven

1. We are regularly encouraged by our newspaper to "attend the church of your choice" on Sunday. How do you think Paul, Peter, or Jude would respond to such an invitation?

2. How are desires like weeds?

3. What is meant by the phrase *"epithumia*-trap?"

4. After reading this chapter, how would you describe/define Paganism?

5. What is the Christian's answer to sinful desires?

Close Encounters of the Spiritual Kind

We have seen that our enemy works within us and among us. Now we must keep reminding ourselves that our battle is not ultimately against flesh and blood. Otherwise, in an effort to promote truth, we attack our own POW's and MIA's. The real war is a spiritual battle for the minds of men. In describing this war zone, the Scripture also describes as enemies those who live by the will of the enemy. As surely as Spirit-filled Christians have the mind of Christ, so also our enemies have the mind of Satan. Just as we are sons of God through faith in Christ, so also those who oppose us are sons of the enemy through faith in anti-Christ. As surely as the Scripture says, "You are gods,"[1] we will soon see that the Scripture also says, "They are enemies."[2] This does not change the fact that there is only One God and only one enemy, but emphasizes that we are controlled by one or the other.

Our Enemy Waits for
Us to Give Him an Opportunity

Our real enemy is constantly on the lookout for easy victims. Peter provides us with insight as to how Satan lies in wait to take over our thoughts for his own purposes. He warns us to "Be self-controlled and alert. Your enemy the devil prowls around like a roaring lion looking for someone to devour. Resist him standing firm in the faith . . . ."[3]

Is the devil hungry and looking for sustenance? Hardly. The

word used by Peter can certainly mean to eat up or devour, to swallow completely in a literal sense. But sometimes it is also quite figurative. For example, the same word is translated in a variety of other ways by the NIV. For example, Paul tells us that:

Death has been swallowed up in victory.[4]

The same word is taken to mean "to be overwhelmed" when Paul tells the Corinthians

"you ought to forgive and comfort him, so that he will not be overwhelmed by excessive sorrow."[5]

In the same letter, Paul describes the result of resurrection in the same terms,

"so that what is mortal may be swallowed up by life."[6]

In the "faith chapter" of Hebrews, we find that the Red Sea "swallowed" the Egyptians. "By faith the people passed through the Red Sea as on dry land; but when the Egyptians tried to do so, they were drowned."[7] When we come back to Peter's warning, couldn't we as well understand that our adversary lies in wait to overwhelm us as a lion overwhelms its victim? Have you ever felt overwhelmed by thoughts you knew were not Godly? When we let up on our control, when we are not alert to the schemes of the enemy, we are open to his jumping right in to overwhelm us with encouragements to ungodly thinking.

Our Enemy Attacks From Close Range

Remember what Jesus said about the essence of his mission being division with respect to the world system?

Do not suppose that I have come to bring peace to the earth. I did not come to bring peace, but a sword. For I have come to turn a man against his father, a daughter against her mother, a daughter-in-law against her mother-in-law—a man's enemies will be the members of his own household.[8]

Jesus warned that our opposition would come through people closest to us. Here's where it's so important to remember that our battle is not with flesh and blood. Since the enemy comes so often through people, it's easy to confuse our fellow victims for the enemy himself. In fact, that is exactly his intent. As long as he can keep the army of Jesus at war with flesh and blood, he is winning the real conflict. As long as we are kept busy at the wrong front, the enemy can advance unhindered.

What we need to learn is how to recognize the influence of the enemy in our family, friends, and co-workers. Our defense is not against our relatives and associates, but against the schemes of the enemy at work in people to keep us and them from experience and knowledge of the truth of God. Paul was describing the kind of opposition to the knowledge of the truth which we would encounter in the last days when he wrote:

> But mark this: There will be terrible times in the last days. People will be lovers of themselves, lovers of money, boastful, proud, abusive, disobedient to their parents, ungrateful, unholy, without love, unforgiving, slanderous, without self-control, brutal, not lovers of the good, treacherous, rash, conceited, lovers of pleasure rather than lovers of God— having a form of godliness but denying its power. Have nothing to do with them. They are the kind who worm their way into homes and gain control over weak-willed women, who are loaded down with sins and are swayed by all kinds of evil desires, always learning but never able to acknowledge the truth. Just as Jannes and Jambres opposed Moses, so also these men oppose the truth— men of depraved minds, who, as far as the faith is concerned, are rejected. But they will not get very far because, as in the case of those men, their folly will be clear to everyone.[8]

Mental Malfunction = Depraved Mind

It is the *nous* of men which is here said to be depraved. This word translated "depravity" is used only here in the New Testament. In the active voice, it generally means to destroy, ruin, or corrupt. Paul uses the term in the passive voice. In other Greek literature, the term apparently means "to be destroyed," "to be ruined," or "to become useless." In at least one context, it seems to be best translated "to be injured." Given the context in Paul's thought, I suspect that each of these ideas is applicable to some degree. Minds are being ruined by evil behavior. Minds become useless as far as the truth is concerned. They have effectively been injured in such a way as to seriously malfunction. The mental *malfunction* common to our times is such that one could say many minds are being destroyed.

Paul discusses this same concept in his letter to the Colossians when he reminds believers that, "Once you were alienated from God and were enemies in your minds because of your evil behavior."[10] Please notice that each of us was at some time among those whose minds were alienated from God. Each of us has been the victim of deception, mental malfunction, and depravity. In the Greek text, the state of enmity is said to be *en*, or "in, with or by" evil behavior. One Kailer *ad hoc* translation of this same passage reads this way, "You were alienated, enemies by intent and purpose while you persisted in evil behavior." When you read the whole context of this discussion in Colossians, you can see that this alienation is in contrast with the state of reconciliation in Christ. In other words, this alienation, the enmity in intent and purpose, is a "normal" pre-reconciled state of all men. It suggests that the enmity is not necessarily the cause, symptom or result of evil behavior, but a corresponding condition which is in effect as long as our purpose is other than the purpose of God for us.

The word which the NIV translates "minds" is the Greek word *dianoia* which we previously encountered. The meaning can range from mind or understanding to purpose, intent, or attitude. The watershed issue in determining whether a man is reconciled to God or alienated from God, an enemy or a friend, is whether that man has chosen to embrace God's design and purpose for himself or is intent on fulfilling some other purpose. The purpose of a man controls the output of his life just as certainly as the purpose or programming of a seed controls what will grow when the seed is planted, therefore the connection between the alienation Paul describes and the evil behavior of pre-reconciled man.

Four Soils, Two Sowers, Two Seeds

Jesus spoke of a similar relationship between seed and fruit when he taught the parables of the sower and the seed. In the first parable, he observes the condition of the soil and the likelihood of a harvest. In the second parable, he clarifies that not all seed is good, but that evil can grow as well as good in prepared soil. Let's just read these two parables and then consider the implications for our study.

Then he told them many things in parables, saying:

"A farmer went out to sow his seed. As he was scattering the seed, some fell along the path, and the birds came and ate it up. Some fell on rocky places, where it did not have much soil. It sprang up quickly, because the soil was shallow. But when the sun came up, the plants were scorched, and they withered because they had no root. Other seed fell among thorns, which grew up and choked the plants. Still other seed fell on good soil, where it produced a crop— a hundred, sixty or thirty times what was sown. He who has ears, let him hear."[10]

Then later in the same chapter, Jesus tells his disciples:

Listen then to what the parable of the sower means: When anyone hears the message about the kingdom and does not understand it, the evil one comes and snatches away what was sown in his heart. This is the seed sown along the path. The one who received the seed that fell on rocky places is the man who hears the word and at once receives it with joy. But since he has no root, he lasts only a short time. When trouble or persecution comes because of the word, he quickly falls away. The one who received the seed that fell among the thorns is the man who hears the word, but the worries of this life and the deceitfulness of wealth choke it, making it unfruitful. But the one who received the seed that fell on good soil is the man who hears the word and understands it. He produces a crop, yielding a hundred, sixty or thirty times what was sown.[12]

We have so often heard sermons and lessons on the importance of being receptive to the Word of God. But how many times has the preacher gone on to warn of the dangers of being prepared to cultivate the wrong message? Jesus continues in the same chapter:

> The kingdom of heaven is like a man who sowed good seed in his field. But while everyone was sleeping, his enemy came and sowed weeds among the wheat, and went away. When the wheat sprouted and formed heads, then the weeds also appeared.
> The owner's servants came to him and said, 'Sir, didn't you sow good seed in your field? Where then did the weeds come from?'
> "'An enemy did this,' he replied.
> "The servants asked him, 'Do you want us to go and pull them up?'
> "'No,' he answered, 'because while you are pulling the weeds, you may root up the wheat with them. Let both grow together until the harvest. At that time I will tell the harvesters: First collect the weeds and tie them in bundles to be burned, then gather the wheat and bring it into my barn.'"[13]

This parable follows the parable of the sower. This good field of wheat is that good soil which is targeted by the enemy. The same good soil for the Word of God (the life of the believer) is full of nourishment for the word of the devil. Somehow we have been deceived into believing that an openness to the reality of the spirit realm and a receptivity to revelation is the whole key to being a Spirit-led Christian. I believe that Jesus is teaching that the same openness which allows the operation of God can serve as a seed-bed for the working of the Accuser if we allow the wrong programming to take root in our lives. I believe the Scripture makes plain that if we attempt to grow a spiritual experience according to our desires and purposes, we may wind up with a plot of devilish weeds rather than a holy garden to the Lord.

Is the weed-infested plot to be rejected or destroyed? Not too soon! Each of us has borne our share of weeds. The heavenly gardener broke us up and plowed our soil that good seed might yet be planted. Our perceived enemies are merely good people who have ingested the wrong seed. If they were not relatively good soil, they would have just been merely nice, benign people who stood for nothing in particular. The very fact that the enemy took advantage of them would alone suggest that they are potentially valuable prospects for restoration to the Creator's purpose.

The Worse They Are, The Better They Can Be

Isn't this is exactly what is illustrated by the life of the Apostle Paul? He was the most vicious enemy of the early Christians, and is forever remembered as the Apostle to the Gentiles, the chief agent of salvation to the western world. Recall what Paul himself said about his past in Judaism:

> I too was convinced that I ought to do all that was possible to oppose the name of Jesus of Nazareth. And that is just what I did in Jerusalem. On the authority of the chief priests I put many of the saints in prison, and when they were put to death, I cast my vote against them. Many a time I went from one synagogue to another to have them punished, and I tried to force them to blaspheme. In my obsession against them, I even went to foreign cities to persecute them.[14]

And in reflection, he writes in a letter to his disciple, Timothy:

> I thank Christ Jesus our Lord, who has given me strength, that he considered me faithful, appointing me to his service. Even though I was once a blasphemer and a persecutor and a violent man, I was shown mercy because I acted in ignorance and unbelief. The grace of our Lord was poured out on me abundantly, along with the faith and love that are in Christ Jesus.[15]

And he went on to say that he really was a model for all times for every enemy of the Gospel who might be recovered for God's purposes:

> Here is a trustworthy saying that deserves full acceptance: Christ Jesus came into the world to save sinners— of whom I am the worst. But for that very reason I was shown mercy so that in me, the worst of sinners, Christ Jesus might display his unlimited patience as an example for those who would believe on him and receive eternal life. Now to the King eternal, immortal, invisible, the only God, be honor and glory for ever and ever. Amen.[16]

Endnotes for Chapter 8

1. John 10:34, quoting Psalms 82:6
2. Matthew 10-:34-36; 2 Timothy 3:1-9; Philippians 3:18.
3. 1 Peter 5:8-9a
4. 1 Corinthians 15:54, quoting Isaiah 25:8
5. 2 Corinthians 2:7
6. 2 Corinthians 5:4
7. Hebrews 11:29
8. Matthew 10:34-36, quoting Micah 7:6
9. 2 Timothy 3:1-9
10. Colossians 1:21
11. Matthew 13:3-9
12. Matthew 13:18-23
13. Matthew 13:24-30
14. Acts 26:9-11
15. 1 Timothy 1:12-14
16. 1 Timothy 1:15-17

Discussion Questions for Chapter Eight

1. If every believer was, at one time, the victim of deception, how can a Christian ever be certain he has really escaped deception?

2. Thinking in terms of wheat and weeds on a personal level, most of us would agree we have borne our share of weeds. Name some of the weeds which might threaten God's wheat in your life.

3. How is our battle really directed toward the schemes of the enemy and not toward people?

4. Describe how minds can become useless as far as the truth is concerned.

Restoring Those Entrapped by the Enemy

If you just think for a moment about where we've been, you can see that God truly cannot save anyone but an enemy. Who ever needed to be reconciled to a friend? The Scripture makes a major point about the love of God in that his love is expressed to those who oppose and resist him.

> You see, at just the right time, when we were still powerless, Christ died for the ungodly. Very rarely will anyone die for a righteous man, though for a good man someone might possibly dare to die. But God demonstrates his own love for us in this: While we were still sinners, Christ died for us. Since we have now been justified by his blood, how much more shall we be saved from God's wrath through him! For if, when we were God's enemies, we were reconciled to him through the death of his Son, how much more, having been reconciled, shall we be saved through his life![1]

Paul never was the enemy, but an enemy pawn. His rescue or call it what you will, his deliverance, conversion, salvation, and/or restoration, broke the enemy's authority and made him a useful servant of the master. You and I have nothing about which to boast before God, either. Except for his kindness, we'd be outcasts without hope. In the same way, the only hope for the present day enemies of God is the love and kindness expressed by the Ambassadors for Christ, who we are. Our warfare strategy (the demolition of strongholds) is to be executed with the objective of reconciling the alienated ones through a new experiential knowledge of the God who is love, living through his redeemed ones. When we are victorious in conflict, even our enemies win!

The Opposition Needs Education

The Apostle Paul was unambiguous when he gave Timothy detailed instructions on how to deal with the opposition. I think I've heard almost every kind of advice about dealing with opposition except the advice given by Paul himself. We've been told to ignore people who resisted us, to shame them, to blast them, to fight them, and who knows what else. Paul told Timothy to teach them. More than this he told him how to teach and why:

> Flee the evil desires of youth, and pursue righteousness, faith, love and peace, along with those who call on the Lord out of a pure heart. Don't have anything to do with foolish and stupid arguments, because you know they produce quarrels. And the Lord's servant must not quarrel; instead, he must be kind to everyone, able to teach, not resentful. Those who oppose him he must gently instruct, in the hope that God will grant them repentance leading them to a knowledge of the truth, and that they will come to their senses and escape from the trap of the devil, who has taken them captive to do his will.[2]

First, don't quarrel. Remember we are representing One whose character is preeminently love and kindness. Our willingness to teach must express kindness and presupposes preparation to clearly and accurately state our case. Our instruction must be without resentment and has to be with gentleness. Anyone who has tried to share the truth of God as Creator and Redeemer with someone steeped in philosophical naturalism, such as Darwinism, will know that *gentleness* is indispensable to gaining a hearing. We are to teach in hope, that is, we are to expect God to bring them to a change of mind. Last, or maybe first, the spiritual warrior must recognize that the opposing one is a captive of the real adversary and we come not to threaten him, but to free him. As Jesus himself declared to be evidence of the Spirit upon him, we proclaim liberty for the captives.

This kind of warfare, the real stuff that really engages the strategy and forces of the enemy is not kid's stuff. To engage in authentic spiritual warfare is to accept the responsibility for the minds of men and the challenge of reconciliation to the plan of the Creator. Further, it can only accomplish God's purposes when we are clothed with divine power in the Holy Spirit.

Another Challenge

One of the most troubling hindrances to bringing conviction and subsequent liberation to the captives in the world is the open displays of spiritual captivity within the church. To this point we've been applying the real work of warfare to the outsider, the person who has been living in utter darkness. It's another task altogether, but no less delicate or challenging (or necessary) to fight the prince of darkness within the ranks of the redeemed. In short, some church members (including family members and friends) live like enemies. When they do, they not only make it more difficult for us to be a united force, but every time one of us chooses to live according to the pattern of the adversary, we give an excuse to the captives to doubt the reality or the value of the deliverance we announce. Paul had this to say about the internal inconsistency of the Christian army:

> For, as I have often told you before and now say again even with tears, many live as enemies of the cross of Christ. Their destiny is destruction, their god is their stomach, and their glory is in their shame. Their mind is on earthly things.[3]

Scripture and experience make it plain that a Christian can choose to become an enemy of God by befriending the world and its values. That is why James also says: "You adulterous people, don't you know that friendship with the world is hatred toward God? Anyone who chooses to be a friend of the world becomes an enemy of God."[4] Is this different than simply conforming for the sake of pseudo-peace? True peace comes only when unity in Christ brings harmony of purpose and action among men. Remember Paul's admonition in Romans 12:1 to stop conforming to the world. Catering to the world's values only condemns the world and cripples the church. Surely, it is a respect for the world's value system which causes the sharpest disputes within the church family itself. When God calls us to holiness, he is calling us to conformity to his values and his standards and at the same time demands the rejection of every alternate value system.

Commitment to God's Purpose: Holiness

We all know there is opposition to the Gospel in the church. We all know there is opposition to righteousness within each of us. But I fear that most who call themselves Christians have never taken seriously the problems they cause by neglecting the discipline of holiness. We saw in chapter 7 that the chief causes of problems among us and within us are natural human desires and appetites. What is the answer? The answer is in learning to keep thoughts captive for Christ, to maintain our minds according to God's will.

How can we practice this mental maintenance? Paul tells the Romans to "be transformed by the renewing of your mind. Then you will be able to test and approve what God's will is—his good, pleasing, and perfect will."[5]

He also tells the Colossians a very practical exercise for mind control:

> Since, then, you have been raised with Christ, set your hearts on things above, where Christ is seated at the right hand of God. Set your minds on things above, not on earthly things. For you died, and your life is now hidden with Christ in God. When Christ, who is your life, appears, then you also will appear with him in glory. Put to death, therefore, whatever belongs to your earthly nature: sexual immorality, impurity, lust, evil desires and greed, which is idolatry. Because of these, the wrath of God is coming. You used to walk in these ways, in the life you once lived. But now you must rid yourselves of all such things as these: anger, rage, malice, slander, and filthy language from your lips. Do not lie to each other, since you have taken off your old self with its practices and have put on the new self, which is being renewed in knowledge in the image of its Creator.[6]

As with capturing an enemy soldier, the only way to do it is to do it. Capturing a thought for Christ is a matter of willfully choosing to snatch a thought from enemy control or domination to surrender it to the authority of Christ. In this Colossians passage, Paul tells us to deliberately set our minds on things above. That ought to keep us from harboring romantic fantasies about the world system. But it's not only a matter of catching runaway thoughts. As we practice living the new life in Christ, we experience stage-by-stage the dynamic and real transformation which comes through knowledge (science—true experiential knowledge). What knowledge? Knowledge of the reality of the life in Christ, the daily warfare of the believer, and the guaranteed victory over the enemy through the power of God.

"Oh, is that all there is?"

Well, no one said it was simple, but don't be discouraged. If you think it all depends on you, you're right. But if you think you can do it in your strength, you're dead wrong! In chapter 10, we're going to see the details of the provisions God has made for our deliverance from the control of sin and death and for the maintenance of our freedom. Remember, this is an ongoing fight, and your adversary, the devil, is still prowling. You need to know that your Deliverer has really set you free and that he intends to keep you free.

Endnotes for Chapter 9

1. Romans 5:6-10
2. 2 Timothy 2:22-26
3. Philippians 3:18-19
4. James 4:4
5. Romans 12:2
6. Colossians 3:1-10

Discussion Questions for Chapter Nine

1. If those who oppose the work of God in you are in need of education, who is to teach them?

2. How does our love for our enemies figure into God's plan for restoration?

3. Can a Christian become an enemy of God?

4. What does Paul mean by "Don't leave anything to do with foolish and stupid arguments"?

5. In what ways does catering to the world's values cripple the church?

CHAPTER TEN

Biblical Deliverance and Freedom

"Ministry of Deliverance." What does that mean? I've heard of deliverance ministries and I've heard different descriptions of what they do. One deliverance ministry specializes in exorcisms. Another claims that both healing and driving our demons is what is meant by deliverance. I suppose that these are the most common slants on what deliverance means.

Let's try another proposition. Could it be that deliverance is what a deliverer does? According to one lexicon, the act of deliverance is to "rescue, save, deliver or preserve someone from someone or something."[1] The implication is that anyone in danger of harm from any cause is a prospect for deliverance.

Jesus, The Deliverer

Jesus is *The Deliverer*. What does Jesus do? Jesus was known as a healer. He cast out demons and raised the dead. But more than anything, Jesus was known by his contemporaries as "Rabbi," Teacher. The Gospels contain about sixty examples of Jesus being called a teacher or referring to himself as a teacher. Even when we find Jesus healing or casting out demons, we see him authenticating his authority as teacher or demonstrating the lessons he taught. Perhaps we would do well to understand a ministry of deliverance as that work of teaching people how to think rightly about the Kingdom of God and to know and trust the power of The King.

The Anointing

Early in Jesus' ministry, he declared himself to be the fulfillment of the prophecy of Isaiah regarding the coming Anointed One. Isaiah's prophecy declared the presence of the Spirit of the Lord evidenced by the anointing to accomplish a specific work.

> The Spirit of the Lord is on me, because he has anointed me to preach good news to the poor. He has sent me to proclaim freedom for the prisoners and recovery of sight for the blind, to release the oppressed, to proclaim the year of the Lord's favor.[2]

How do we know that the Spirit of the Lord is on Jesus? Because he has been anointed (this is the verbal form of the noun "Christ") to preach, to proclaim, to liberate, and to preach some more. Preaching and proclaiming are both some form of teaching, and liberation is a result of correct instruction.

Knowledge and Liberation

Jesus himself taught that correct knowledge was the key to liberation. Listen to the place of learning and knowledge in this often partially quoted passage from the Gospel of John:

> Jesus said, "If you hold to my teaching, you are really my disciples. Then you will know the truth, and the truth will set you free."
> They answered him, "We are Abraham's descendants and have never been slaves of anyone. How can you say that we shall be set free?"
> Jesus replied, "I tell you the truth, everyone who sins is a slave to sin. Now a slave has no permanent place in the family, but a son belongs to it forever. So if the Son sets you free, you will be free indeed."[3]

The true student of Jesus is the one who lives, dwells, and abides in the message of Jesus. It is in this life-style learned from the Master Teacher that the disciple experiences reality. This experiential knowledge of genuine reality, truth, is the key to freedom. This word for freedom is the same word used elsewhere for deliverance, liberation or being set free.

It is worthy of note that the Jews to whom Jesus was speaking were not deliberately the enemies of God. They saw themselves as children of Abraham, the select people of God. Yet, Jesus clearly identified them as in bondage. Their bondage was neither sickness nor demonic oppression. The bondage from which they needed deliverance was an attitude about the substance of authentic sin, righteousness, and judgment. They thought sin was disobedience to the traditions of the elders. Genuine sin is unconformity to the purposes of God. They thought righteousness was found in conformity to their religious system. Genuine righteousness is found only in conformity to the purposes of God in spite of the rules and expectations of religious people. They believed judgment would be on the basis of biological relationship to the recipient of the ancient promise. We who have experienced deliverance know that judgment is only on the basis of relationship to the Lawgiver and Judge.

Experiencing Daily Deliverance

You will remember that James tells us that temptation comes from our own desire. We have already seen that the way we control or fail to control our thoughts is the essence of this battle for the mind. We need to ask God for daily liberation from the thoughts and fleshly desires which produce temptation. Isn't this daily deliverance really the same principle as the life-style of freedom which we read about in other New Testament passages?

The Life-style of Freedom

Paul writes to the Romans what may be the most thorough discourse on the life-style of freedom. This kind of freedom belongs only to the one who has accepted deliverance in Christ. Let's read this selection together, then see just how it relates to our study.

> . . . where sin increased, grace increased all the more, so that, just as sin reigned in death, so also grace might reign through righteousness to bring eternal life through Jesus Christ our Lord.

What shall we say, then? Shall we go on sinning so that grace
may increase?

By no means! We died to sin; how can we live in it any longer? Or
don't you know that all of us who were baptized into Christ Jesus
were baptized into his death? We were therefore buried with him
through baptism into death in order that, just as Christ was raised
from the dead through the glory of the Father, we too may live a
new life.

If we have been united with him like this in his death, we will
certainly also be united with him in his resurrection. For we know
that our old self was crucified with him so that the body of sin might
be done away with, that we should no longer be slaves to sin—
because anyone who has died has been freed from sin.

Now if we died with Christ, we believe that we will also live with
him. For we know that since Christ was raised from the dead, he
cannot die again; death no longer has mastery over him. The death
he died, he died to sin once for all; but the life he lives, he lives to
God.

Paul goes on to explain how we should live this new life:

In the same way, count yourselves dead to sin but alive to God in
Christ Jesus. Therefore do not let sin reign in your mortal body so
that you obey its evil desires. Do not offer the parts of your body to
sin, as instruments of wickedness, but rather offer yourselves to
God, as those who have been brought from death to life; and offer
the parts of your body to him as instruments of righteousness. For
sin shall not be your master, because you are not under law, but
under grace.

What then? Shall we sin because we are not under law but under
grace? By no means! Don't you know that when you offer yourselves
to someone to obey him as slaves, you are slaves to the one whom
you obey—whether you are slaves to sin, which leads to death, or to
obedience, which leads to righteousness? But thanks be to God that,
though you used to be slaves to sin, you wholeheartedly obeyed the
form of teaching to which you were entrusted. You have been set
free from sin and have become slaves to righteousness.

And somewhat condescendingly, Paul continues,

I put this in human terms because you are weak in your natural
selves. Just as you used to offer the parts of your body in slavery to
impurity and to ever-increasing wickedness, so now offer them
in slavery to righteousness leading to holiness.

> When you were slaves to sin, you were free from the control
> of righteousness. What benefit did you reap at that time from
> the things you are now ashamed of? Those things result in
> death! But now that you have been set free from sin and have
> become slaves to God, the benefit you reap leads to holiness,
> and the result is eternal life. For the wages of sin is death, but
> the gift of God is eternal life in Christ Jesus our Lord.[4]

Paul was declaring the universal possibility of redemption
through the kindness of God expressed in Jesus Christ. Since
the grace of God is greater than the disobedience of man, Paul
says that if sin increases, grace increases, so that the possibility of restoration still exists even in the worst setting. Some-
body hearing the message evidently had a *mental malfunction.*
Instead of hearing the good news of the grace of God, someone
heard an opportunity to turn the message of grace into an
excuse for unbridled sin. The malfunctioning mind reasons this
way: "If grace is good, more grace is better. If more sin means
more grace, then we need to sin as much as possible to receive
the maximum amount of God's grace." I call this a mental
malfunction, since it is a *non sequitur, i.e.,* the conclusion does
not follow from the premise. Worse, the conclusion contradicts
the context. Paul is declaring deliverance and freedom from
sin, not deliverance from judgment and freedom to sin. Paul's
response to this mental malfunction is to teach. Those who had
experienced deliverance in Christ were headed for bondage to
sin by means of a misunderstanding of the nature of the deliverance itself. The pivotal statement in this passage, as far as
our discussion is concerned, is in verse eleven: "Count yourselves dead to sin . . . ."

Here we find the means to make this theoretical freedom our
possession in experience as well as in theology. The term
"count" is the Greek word *logizomai,* related to the semantic
family including words like the noun and logic, or verbs like
reason, consider, think, suppose, maintain, claim, think on or
reflect upon. In an earlier chapter, we discussed the word *logismos,* also related to "count," meaning thinking or reasoning.
The deliverance from sin by God's grace is our possession and
experience as we take our thoughts captive for Christ. We
maintain the daily walk of freedom as these thoughts remain

controlled by the Spirit of life rather than by sin, because, "through Christ Jesus the law [system] of the Spirit of life set me free from the law [system] of sin and death."

When we turn to the Galatian Epistle, we see a plain case study in maintaining freedom. The question of freedom versus bondage is at stake. The choice is one between different teachers and contrary doctrines. The Apostle Paul had taught freedom from the system of law controlled by sin and death. Liberation had been declared through faith in Jesus Christ. Now, however, "some people are throwing [the Christians] into confusion and are trying to pervert the gospel of Christ."[5]

Paul describes a particular conflict in Galatia this way: "Some false brothers had infiltrated our ranks to spy on the freedom we have in Christ Jesus and to make us slaves." Paul continues with his response to these false teachers, "We did not give in to them for a moment, so that the truth of the gospel might remain with you."[6] Later in Galatians, Paul writes one of my favorite summaries of the Gospel of deliverance and freedom: "It is for freedom that Christ has set us free. Stand firm, then, and do not let yourselves be burdened again by a yoke of slavery."[7]

We experience deliverance from bondage through hearing and embracing the truth of the Gospel. We maintain our freedom by guarding our hearts and minds from the deceitfulness of false teaching and its fruits. We must take a stand for truth and stand firm. Freedom was deliberately provided by Christ and only our deliberate maintenance will preserve it.

Endnotes for Chapter 10

1. Arndt & Gingrich, *A Greek-English Lexicon of the New Testament and Other Early Christian Literature, 1957.*
2. Luke 4:18-19, quoting Isaiah 61:1-2
3. John 8:31-36
4. Romans 5:20b-6:23
5. Galatians 1:7
6. Galatians 2:4-5
7. Galatians 5:1

Discussion Questions for Chapter Ten

1. How does Paul's epistle to the Galatians provide a case study in maintaining freedom?

2. What is required of any person who desires to experience fully the liberation discussed in John 8?

3. Why care about deliverance ministry?

4. What is the connection between a ministry of deliverance and spiritual warfare?

CHAPTER ELEVEN

Our Struggle

I can remember one day several years ago when the thought occurred to me that I had never questioned whether I was truly saved until after I was truly converted. How strange. I was fairly confident, well assured of my life in Christ before that day. To be genuinely converted, one must come to grips with the fact of his lostness. This I understood. But why should the insecurity arise after I had the promise of eternal life?

Well, I had been deceived before. Could I have been deceived when I embraced the Gospel? Had I been baptized in vain? I remember it was such a struggle, such a struggle as I had never known before.

I knew that I took the biblical promises at face value. My new found faith was firmly planted on Scripture. Formerly my assurance was based on trust in my personal essential goodness and belief in the myth that our family was a "covenant" family, whatever that meant.

Actually, the doubts and insecurities I had discovered turned out not to be my exclusive possession. Others admitted they had a similar experience. I soon confirmed the truth of Peter's assurance that my "brothers throughout the world are undergoing the same kind of sufferings." Interesting that in the middle of this talk of suffering Peter would add, "that this is the true grace of God. Stand fast in it."[1] It sounds like Peter expected difficulties to be encountered by Christians.

Paul said exactly that in his seond letter to Timothy. He writes, "In fact, everyone who wants to live a godly life in Christ Jesus will be persecuted . . . ."[2] It seems as though there are forces at work in an effort to produce dissatisfaction with the Christian life. Could it be . . . ?

My study into this question led me to believe that there are both internal and external forces to which we will respond. The trials are not necessarily different for Christians, but our responses take on a whole new importance.

Paul tells us that "we know that in all things God works for the good of those who love him, who have been called according to his purpose."[3] I was beginning to suspect that in the same way, Satan works for the undoing of those who fear him, who listen to his call and conform to his purpose. Apparently, the enemy within us can invite us to think thoughts contrary to truth.

When I consider Job, I am reminded that bad things do happen to good people. God himself calls Job righteous. In fact, this is the very reason for Satan to desire his testing. If Satan can just get Job to turn from his righteousness because of pressure, Satan will prove his point: that the people of God only serve God because of their own selfish interests in so doing. If Satan can get Job to believe that God is somehow responsible for his dilemma, he can claim that Job has abandoned his trust in God. Can you see that indicting God for the unpleasant events of life is also to deny him his honor as Redeemer and Deliverer? How can anyone look to the source of his problems as the answer for his problems? God cannot be both the Savior and the Persecutor of man.

The author of the book of Job reveals his understanding of the nature of the test and Job's victory in it. He wrote, "In all this, Job did not sin by charging God with wrongdoing."[4] Job was an overcomer because he trusted God as his Redeemer and would not think of accusing God as being the source of his trouble.

Once we recognize that a chief strategy in Satan's toolbox is to get the people of God blaming God for their troubles, we have not only a clearer understanding, but a defense for such an attack. The events in Job's life and the attack on his physical health were external forces used by the Devil in an attempt to create doubt in the love of God. Job's friends were then used by Satan to induce deadly thinking. The ideas came from his friends, but once released as fiery darts, they had the potential to burn within him.

It is easy to see how the pressures mounted up against Job,

both from the outside and within. It is just as clear that the Apostle Paul experienced the same suffering. Paul describes his own experience in these words:

> . . . as servants of God we commend ourselves in every way: in great endurance; in troubles, hardships and distresses; in beatings, imprisonments and riots; in hard work, sleepless nights and hunger; in purity, understanding, patience and kindness; in the Holy Spirit and in sincere love; in truthful speech and in the power of God; with weapons of righteousness in the right hand and the left, through glory and dishonor, bad report and good report; genuine, yet regarded as impostors; known, yet regarded as unknown; dying, and yet we live on; beaten, and yet not killed; sorrowful, yet always rejoicing; poor, yet making many rich, having nothing and yet possessing everything.[5]

Please take a few minutes to stop and visualize at least a couple of the situations Paul recounts. From a simply human perspective, you could say he was doing everything right and everything came out wrong. In purity and truthful speech having a bad report? To be considered an impostor since abandoning the hypocrisy of his life in Judaism? Living in understanding, patience, kindness and beatings? What's wrong with this picture?

What injustice! Couldn't a situation like this leave you angry? What was your response the last time you felt slighted? Do you remember a time when you felt like you were being punished for doing well? Perhaps you felt indignation. You might have even been tempted to ask, "How could God allow . . . ?"

Paul described in even greater detail the internal struggle which was his own battle with his flesh nature, as differentiated from his spirit self. Beginning at Romans 7:14 and reading all the way to Romans 8:21, Paul explains how a person could continue to struggle after receiving freedom in Christ. The deliverance and freedom experienced in Jesus liberate the inner man from the administration of sin and death, but the physical nature continues in the world, under the curse, bound by the administration of sin and death, awaiting with the rest of creation the liberation from its bondage to decay.

It is in this ongoing struggle after becoming a Christian that one discovers a whole new meaning for the trials of life. Paul reminds us that the people of Israel during the days of Moses had experienced deliverance, but still fell in unbelief. He says:

> So, if you think you are standing firm, be careful that you don't fall! No temptation has seized you except what is common to man. And God is faithful; he will not let you be tempted beyond what you can not bear. But when you are tempted, he will also provide a way out so that you can stand up under it.[6]

What this means is this, God knew that Job could handle the trials of Job, or Job would have been protected from that degree of testing. When my trials overwhelming, I actually find a source of strength in knowing that God knows what I can handle. As my troubles intensify, I have real evidence that God's faith in me is growing. It is a vote of confidence from God every time the situation inexplicably deteriorates.

I was told that it is not uncommon when studying this area of spiritual warfare for a person to get the enemy's attention, to experience a special *ad hoc* assault to hinder the work of exposing Satan's activity. I really doubted that this could really happen. I was fairly convinced that when a person reported increased affliction while working on this subject that it was just a matter of getting what was expected. You talk enough about contrary spirits and you think everything is the work of a contrary spirit, you know.

Now after months of working on the manuscript for this book, I believe I have witnessed an opposition to this work which I cannot help but to explain in terms of the enemy's fear and anger at being exposed. Like Job and the apostles, my struggle has been both internal and external. I have been hearing every sort of reason why I should not the right man for the job. Every one of my past failures at any endeavor has been resurrected to haunt me and torment me.

My external hindrances have been even more striking. I have had some of the greatest health problems of my life during the past months of giving shape to this book. In 1993 I have already spent seven weeks hospitalized and I am going to be scheduled for another hospital stay with surgery very soon. The doctors are baffled at my symptoms and don't understand what we are dealing with. I originally saw a doctor because of severe pain in my left arm and shoulder. Tests indicated an advanced osteo myelitus, an infection of my left clavicle. (There had been no injury that could have caused this.)

After weeks of treatment with a powerful antibiotic by intravenous infusion, I had a sudden fright night, complete with an emergency blood transfusion—two units of packed red cells). For some unknown reason, I had a dramatic drop in hemoglobin and other physical symptoms. A few days later, a C.A.T. scan exposed a soft tissue mass behind my left clavicle. It was definitely severely restricting blood return to my left arm. The doctors did not have a name for it. One doctor said, "When we get through this, I'm going to write 'The Glenn Kailer Book of Weird Medicine.'"

A needle biopsy of the mass indicated no pathology, no active culture. But continuing C.A.T. scans indicate that the thing is growing quite rapidly. Through this, I have had some of the most intense pain I have ever experienced, and I have also had some of the most brain—numbing drugs I have known. This book is being written in small blocks of time between peaks in pain and doses of narcotics. It would have been easier to drop the project, but not as productive. Will the affliction abate when the work is completed? I certainly hope so! But this I know: "Through your prayers and the help given by the Spirit of Jesus Christ, what has happened to me will turn out for my deliverance."[7]

Endnotes for Chapter 11

1. 1 Peter 5:8-12
2. 2 Timothy 3:12
3. Romans 8:28
4. Job 1:22
5. 2 Corinthians 6:4-10
6. 1 Corinthians 10:12-13
7. Philippians 1:19

Discussion Questions for Chapter Eleven

1. If personal security in salvation is no guarantee of a living relationship with God, what is the basis of confidence for one truly redeemed?

2. Which pressure do you feel more of — the internal or the external?

3. What charge might the Accuser bring on your account?

4. What is there about your life to which God himself could point in your defense when Satan accuses?

5. Why do we know that God is not the source of our problems?

6. What does the enemy achieve if he gets us to doubt the love of God toward each of us, individually and personally?

7. If increasing temptation or pressure comes into my life, what has been/should be my response?

The Missing Word

Have you noticed the missing word in our study of spiritual warfare? Many discussions on the subject of spiritual warfare are, more or less, studies on prayer. When I began my biblical research on spiritual warfare, I discovered quite early that Scripture has much to say about both prayer and spiritual warfare, but not *together*. The closest thing in Scripture to relating prayer to warfare is that familiar passage in Ephesians about praying with your armor in place.

After his description of the Christian soldier's panoply, Paul writes:

And pray in the Spirit on all occasions with all kinds of prayers and requests. With this in mind, be alert and always keep on praying for all the saints.
Pray also for me, that whenever I open my mouth, words may be given me so that I will fearlessly make known the mystery of the gospel, for which I am an ambassador in chains. Pray that I may declare it fearlessly, as I should.[1]

This passage does not identify the war *as* prayer, but it does include praying as part of the preparation for spiritual warfare. We can wreak havoc in the enemy's domain after we've prayed, but not until we've prayed.

Paul tells us to pray in the Spirit, not merely in the will and motivation of the flesh. We are to pray for every warrior in the army of God. In fact, prayer related to warfare is generally a prayer for the army of God, rather than for personal needs. When Paul does present a personal request, it is that he may be better equipped for his share of the war. His prayer is for a sharp sword and uncompromised boldness (a worthwhile prayer for every believer).

A Task as Big as Life

When I think about the warfare we've described, it strikes me that the challenge is enormous. Every fact of existence in this universe intersects God's design and purpose in some way. This elevates every study of truth in any field to a level of some importance. Any truth is subject to suppression and distortion by the adversary and liar, Satan. All truth is God's truth and worthy of our defense.

My life as one system in a universe of human systems is significant because I know that my life is designed by an Almighty Creator who expressed his own likeness when he fashioned my existence. What I do with my life and my mind, my impact on other human systems becomes intensely important if I care at all about conforming to the design of the Creator. I will press on in order that I might share in the glory of a perfectly functioning whole restoration of creation.

Anxiety: Take it or leave it!

Anxiety? When I consider the bigness of my responsibility to every man for my ministry, I could be crippled with fear of failure. But the Apostle Paul tells us that we do not need to suffer such anxiety. In his letter to believers at Philippi, he is talking about his own ability to glorify God in any and every situation, whether by life or by death. He tells of a joy in suffering and reveals the key to endurance: God is at work in us to will and to act according to his purpose.[2] He also tells us to rejoice rather than to struggle with anxiety.[3] We either leave our anxieties at the throne of grace or we take them through life with us.

Paul reveals that we may choose to be guarded by the peace of God or to be enveloped in the turmoil characteristic of the world's chaos. The cares of the world will produce in you a fullness of despair as inexplicable as the peace of God which defies understanding. Is the task great? Sure! But the power of God is adequate for any challenge. His power is at work within us who are surrendered to him such that he wills our wants and does our actions to conform our lives to his purpose. It is in this conformity to God's purpose that we recover meaning and value. It is in this adherence to the design of the Creator that we are being restored to the glory, honor and immortality that is ours by birthright (re-birthright, of course).

We noticed several chapters ago that Jesus is the model for restored humanity. His life revealed a peace which made no sense in the light of his surroundings. His cool before Pontius Pilate is beyond comprehension. His comfortableness, even casualness in driving out evil spirits or raising the dead baffles the mind. What was it which enabled the Savior to do such things while on earth? We read at every major juncture in his ministry that Jesus engaged in an all night prayer vigil. Could we agree that we might be as needful of prayer as the incarnate God himself?

His disciples recognized in Jesus' example that his prayer life was his source of wisdom and strength, power and purpose. It was through his heavenward study that he saw the Father's plan and purpose for the coming hours. His disciples learned from his example the importance of much time in serious prayer. Now they wanted to learn also from him the way, the how-to of effective prayer. They came to Jesus requesting a lesson in the kind of praying which equipped the Savior for spiritual warfare. They asked him to teach them to pray as he prayed. In response to this request he taught them . . .

The Lord's Prayer — The Warrior's Prayer

This, then, is how you should pray: "Our Father in heaven, hallowed be your name, your kingdom come, your will be done on earth as it is in heaven. Give us today our daily bread. Forgive us our debts, as we also have forgiven our debtors. And lead us not into temptation, but deliver us from the evil one."[4]

Is this all that Jesus said when he prayed all night? Isn't it clear that this was his outline for prayer and was never intended to be a specific prayer? This is not the content, but the method of prayer.

The Lord's Prayer is the most often quoted prayer among
Christians. But perhaps you haven't considered its application
to spiritual warfare. Jesus said to pray in this way. So how are
we to pray? I remember the story of the child who had learned
this prayer in Sunday School. His parents asked him what he
had learned that day and he reported that the teacher told
them that God's name was Harold. "The teacher told us to
pray, 'Our Father who art in heaven, Harold be your name.'"

Harold who? Hallowed where? What are we praying for,
exactly? His own desire is to be hallowed in the minds of men,
isn't it? An essential part of restoration in the new creation is
to have men rightly *think* about God and their relationship to
him. May I suggest this become for you more and more a
warrior's prayer, desiring the advancement of the honor of God
in the thinking of people everywhere?

Your kingdom come surely is the battle cry of the warrior. If
we are going to be effective soldiers in the Lord's army, we will
devote every action of our lives to doing and demonstrating the
reign of God. But the prayer is not that we ourselves should
submit (isn't this prayer only expressed by one already in
submission?), but that every other person on earth would
participate in submitting to the doing of God's will. This level
of restoration is not to occur, of course, in this age, but we are
to look forward to its being a reality when Jesus returns.

To pray for daily bread is to pray for our supply needs while
at the battle's front. I had often wondered why we should pray
for daily supply. I mean, why not pray for a weekly supply and
not bother God so often? God desires that we be protected from
self-reliance, one of the greatest of sins. By remaining dependent on God's daily presence, we know we need him every day
of our lives.

I think now of forgiveness as an armor repair and sealant. My
helmet of salvation remains secure only as I am secure in my
relationship to God. My vital spiritual organs have their protection in the covering of righteousness, possible only through
forgiveness. Forgiving and being forgiven have everything to do
with how we think about anyone in any relationship.

The trials of Job, the hassles of the Apostle Paul and even
our own conflicts testify that faith in God is not an escape from

our own conflicts testify that faith in God is not an escape from anything. Receiving the freedom Jesus gives is not the end of conflict. To maintain freedom as our daily lifestyle, forgiveness must be part of our daily experience.

The last thing we must note in the Lord's prayer is that it is clearly not a private prayer. It is directed, not to MY Father, but OUR Father. Give US, forgive US. We are a body, like it or not, and God will deal with us as a body. Of what value is a soldier's victory if his army loses the war? Because I desire to share in the victory, I pray for your victory.

An Author's Prayer

My prayer to Our Father for you, my dear reader, is that his name be increasingly hallowed in your thoughts and conversations. May the name of Jesus be held in high esteem in every human system of which you are a part.

I pray that God be the Ruler and Guide for your life. May the character of Jesus be reproduced in you and may you, always wearing the belt of truth, reproduce the reality of redeemed relationships among the people with whom you live and work. May the kingdom of God be where you are. May God have his way with you in such a way that his beautiful *design* is manifested in and through you as surely as his will is manifested in heaven itself.

I pray that your needs be met in accordance with the fullness of resources at the hand of the Creator. May the flow of resources be adequate that you may sow an abundance of seed by meeting the needs of others. Yet, may the abundance of your supply never obscure your vision and give the enemy opportunity to induce self-reliance.

May the freedom and joy of complete release be yours as you deliberately forgive every offense against you. In the exercise of such forgiveness, may you come to the full riches of complete understanding of God's forgiveness toward you.

May Satan's work as the Accuser of the saints be spoiled and foiled by the way you live and *think* among the people of God. May you be delivered from every form of deception in order that you may prove victorious over the Evil One whose purpose is to distort the knowledge of God.

May you be effective in the use of each part of the armor of God to the pulling down of every stronghold, the demolition of every argument and the exposure of every pretense which is set against the true knowledge of the one and only God who is Truth. May God grant you a share in the victory at the front lines of the battle of the ages. Amen.

Endnotes for Chapter 12

1. Ephesians 6:18-20
2. Philippians 2:13
3. Philippians 4:4-7
4. Matthew 6:9-13 (Some refer to this as the Model Prayer of Jesus and John 17 as the Lord's Prayer.)

Discussion Questions for Chapter Twelve

1. Does the Bible describe our war *as* prayer? Why or why not?

2. Why do you suppose that *every* fact of existence in the universe intersects God's design and purpose?

3. How can we recover meaning and value by conforming to God's purpose?

4. Compare John 17 with what has been called the "Lord's Prayer." How are they alike? How are they different?

5. Why is Jesus' Model Prayer not private?